SECRET ST. LOUIS

A GUIDE TO THE WEIRD, WONDERFUL, AND OBSCURE

David Baugher

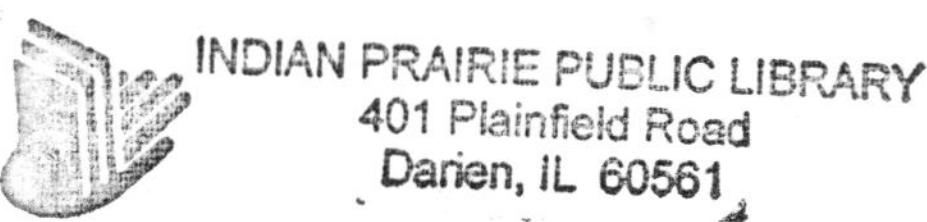

Reedy Press
PO Box 5131
St. Louis, MO 63139
www.reedypress.com

Library of Congress Control Number: 2016931466

ISBN: 9781681060392

Design by Jill Halpin

Printed in the United States of America
16 17 18 19 20   5 4 3 2 1

CONTENTS

INTRODUCTION

My favorite questions about a city are the ones no one ever thinks to ask.

How can I see a cube of a million one-dollar bills downtown? Did Abraham Lincoln almost kill a man in a swordfight in St. Charles County? Do we have a nudist resort in St. Louis? Was a Revolutionary War battle once fought near Busch Stadium? Where can I get a ten-pound apple pie inspired by the Great Flood of 1993? Is there a local hall of fame for dogs? Did St. Louis invent baseball's no-hitter? Why is West County Center represented by a dove? Who started KSHE radio in his suburban basement? Is there a radioactive waste dump where I can have a picnic? Does anyone really know what on earth a "Billiken" actually is? Where is a piece of New York's Twin Towers on display here?

Welcome to *Secret St. Louis*, the things you never even knew you wanted to know about the city we all call home.

If there is a common thread to the odds and ends of this admittedly random work, it is that it examines the area by looking at it through the lens of the unusual. Some of what lies within is comical while some might make you cry. Parts are educational while other parts are useless. From the cute to the creepy, from the sad to the sublime, from the topical to the trivial, this is the side of our town that was under your nose the whole time just waiting to be discovered. Most important of all, it is uniquely St. Louis.

So dive right in to this collection of the unexplored treasures, little-known institutions, hidden history, quirky oddities, unvisited monuments, and offbeat questions to which even lifelong St. Louisans wouldn't normally give much thought. In short, this is a Gateway City scavenger hunt of the stuff you never knew or never thought to ask. Best of all, each of the 97 items within is attached to a site you can visit to experience a bit of the uniquely wonderful culture of this fascinating place for yourself.

1 THE BIG CONE

Why does a South County school have a gigantic ice cream cone out front?

For any youngster, nothing quite beats a cold dairy treat on a hot August day. But even for the chilliest winter afternoons, the children of Mesnier Primary School have a nice reminder of the perks of summer just outside their window. Rising some 18 feet into the air, this South County oddity seems as iconic as it is out of place. What's a giant ice cream cone doing outside a school anyway?

The well-known cone turns out to be a remnant of a now-defunct Velvet Freeze that once plied its trade along Gravois Road. These days Velvet Freeze is but a memory in this part of town. Only one location remains and it is in North County.

But this relic lives on nonetheless. Granted, it may be a bit difficult for the kids to take a bite, but this cone does have one advantage over its smaller and more edible counterparts. It can change flavors with a simple coat of paint. In fact, its present strawberry and chocolate characteristics are the result of coloration added to the original vanilla artwork.

The term "primary" school is no accident. Unlike an elementary school, Mesnier only runs through the second grade.

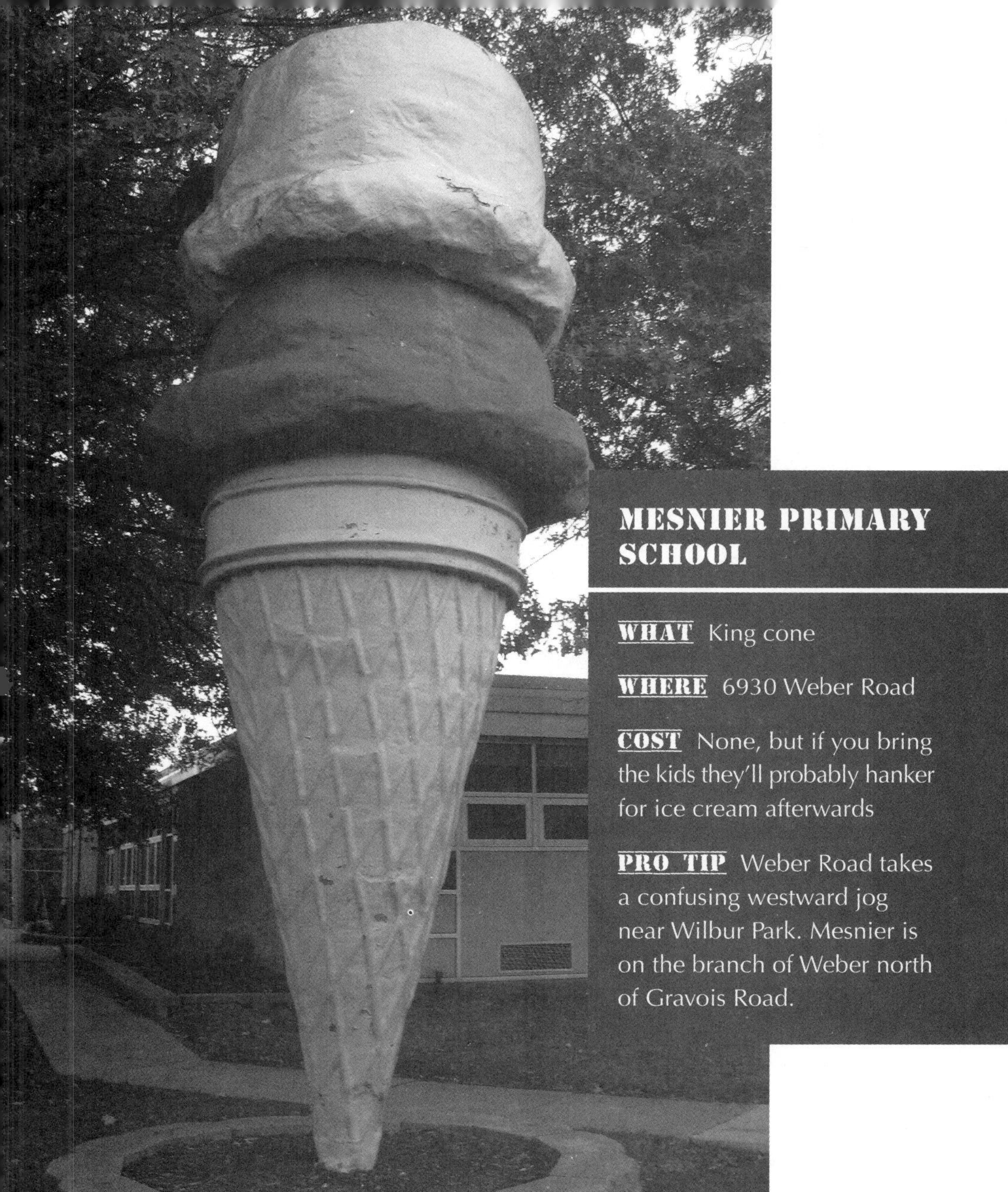

MESNIER PRIMARY SCHOOL

WHAT King cone

WHERE 6930 Weber Road

COST None, but if you bring the kids they'll probably hanker for ice cream afterwards

PRO TIP Weber Road takes a confusing westward jog near Wilbur Park. Mesnier is on the branch of Weber north of Gravois Road.

It takes the power of a child's imagination to envision oneself consuming a cone of such magnitude. The best an adult's imagination can do is probably to try and figure out just how much it would cost if you really bought an ice cream this size.

2 THE PHANTOM FREEWAY

Why is the Chestnut at 20th exit so convoluted?

To many, it is a handy route downtown, but even the most grizzled St. Louis travelers can sometimes find themselves a bit bewildered by the bafflingly tortuous path of I-64's Exit 38B. The perplexingly roomy two-lane egress road winds through not one but two 90-degree turns, swooping beneath Market Street along a strangely winding route before letting out at the intersection of Chestnut and 20th streets. Longer than some downtown streets, the unusual ramp runs more than half a mile by itself. It's also paired to a corresponding entrance to the interstate which runs the other direction from Pine Street that is every bit as inexplicably wide and lengthy as its cousin.

Chestnut Street was originally misspelled "Chesnut" until 1893.

ROUTE 755

WHAT A failed highway turned exit ramp

WHERE Chestnut at 20th exit

COST Only the gas to get there and the sad knowledge of what could have been

PRO TIP You can drive it but there is no stopping. You can park at a Chestnut Street meter and walk back if you like.

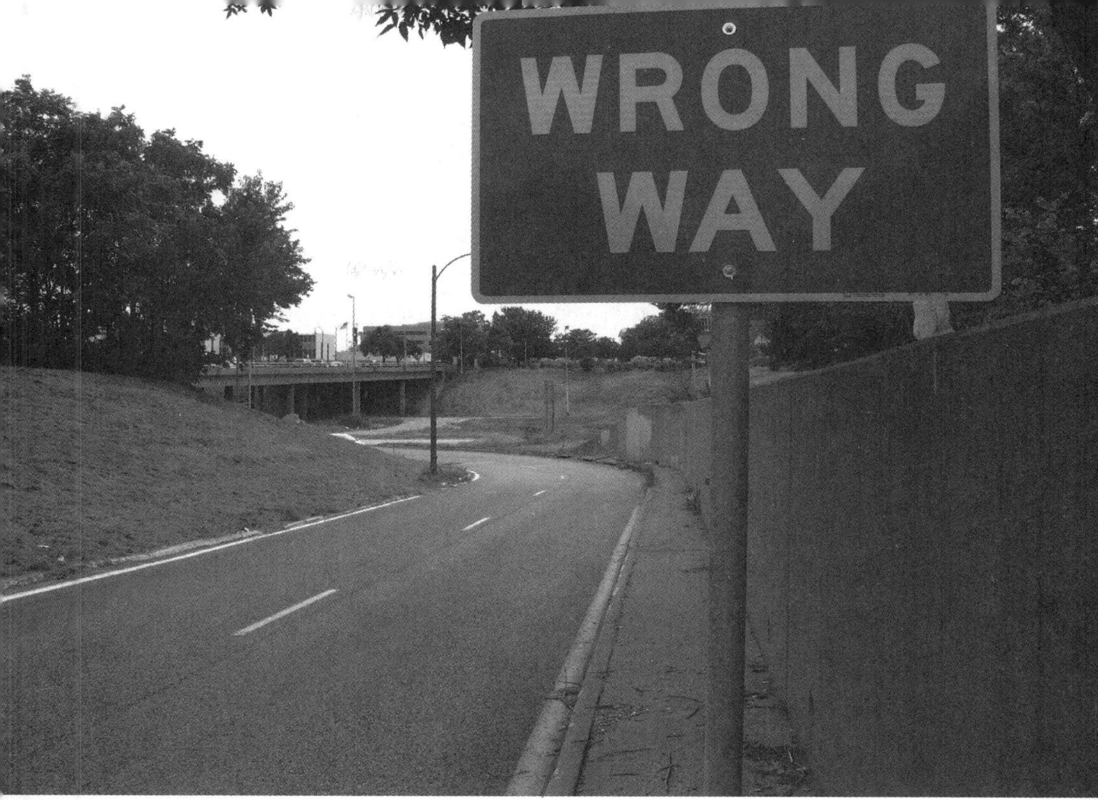

A sign for errant travelers along the half-mile-long ramp echoes the same message the public itself gave to backers of a highway that would have provided a bypass outside downtown.

What keen observers might notice is that this is no ordinary highway exit. In fact, it is the truncated corpse of what was once intended to be a highway all to itself. The proposed north-south distributor, known as Route 755, was intended to connect I-44 to I-70 via a path circling outside downtown. (Ever notice that I-64 eastbound is strangely severed from any downtown interstate link that would keep you from motoring into the Land of Lincoln? Yep, 755 was supposed to fix that.) But by 1980, the long-planned new expressway fell victim to public resistance and renewed interest in neighborhood preservation. Today, the oddly constructed I-44/I-55 flyover and the unnaturally designed Chestnut at 20th Street exit are the last ghostly remains of a long-planned highway that never was.

3 BIGFOOT® HANGS HIS HAT IN PACIFIC

Was monster trucking born in St. Louis?

When St. Louis couple Bob Chandler and his wife Marilyn bought an F-250 in 1974 to indulge their passion for off-roading, there wasn't much to distinguish the vehicle.

Little did they know that they had just purchased what would become the most famous pickup on the planet—BIGFOOT, the vehicle that would spawn an entirely new American pastime. The following year, the pair and a neighbor opened a parts and service operation for 4x4s and began using—and augmenting—their truck for personal off-roading while displaying it at local car shows and tractor pulls. By the beginning of the following decade, the vehicle's iconic oversized tires made it so widely known that it was becoming an industry in itself, appearing in commercials, TV shows, and even a movie.

BIGFOOT® 4X4, INC.

WHAT The world's first monster truck

WHERE 2286 Rose Lane, Pacific, Mo.

COST None

NOTEWORTHY With 10-foot tires, BIGFOOT 5 became the Guinness record holder for the tallest and widest pickup truck in the world.

The name BIGFOOT® wasn't a reference to the size of the vehicle's famous tires. It was actually a nickname for Bob Chandler due to his fondness for the truck's gas pedal.

Interestingly, no one initially thought of BIGFOOT's signature stunt—crushing cars—until 1981, when Bob Chandler tried the experiment in a cornfield in front of a small but appreciative group. At first, he didn't even want to do it in public for fear it would make his beloved truck seem destructive.

Today, BIGFOOT has any number of imitators, and the company Chandler founded has since created a fleet of 20 monster trucks of its own. Yet, the granddaddy of them all still exists at BIGFOOT's new headquarters in Pacific, Missouri, where it relocated from Hazelwood in 2015. Various BIGFOOT trucks are slated to ultimately be on display there once the four-decade-old company gets settled in.

But one thing is for sure.

BIGFOOT, the truck that created an industry, is a St. Louisan.

BIGFOOT
Used with permission by BIGFOOT 4x4, Inc.

BIGFOOT, The Original Monster Truck®, is both an American original and a St. Louis native.

4 THE BIZARRE BATTLE OF HERMANN

How did a handful of men try to hold off an army with one gun?

Missouri represented a fertile and chaotic theater of combat during the American Civil War. Significant fighting occurred here, with a number of vital skirmishes being crucial to control of the border state.

The very strange Battle of Hermann was definitely not one of them.

It all started with "Price's Raid," a meandering and ultimately fruitless effort to break the Union's hold on the Midwest. The doomed attempt began when the Confederates sent ex-Missouri Governor Sterling Price back to reinvade his home state, with the original plan being to push through to St. Louis. However, Price found that the Gateway City was too well protected and shifted west, which is what brought his forces to the sleepy little river town of Hermann.

HERMANN'S HISTORIC CANNON

WHAT The little cannon that could

WHERE 119 E. 1st Street, Hermann, Mo.

COST Free

NOTEWORTHY Price's Raid resulted in little fighting around St. Louis itself despite that being its original target. The campaign was eventually repulsed at the Battle of Westport fought in October 1864. It was the last big Southern offensive in Missouri.

This tiny cannon still stands watch as the gun that "saved" Hermann for its key role in one of the less strategically vital battles of the American Civil War.

In an underwhelming display of gallantry, most of Hermann's defenders abandoned their posts and headed for the hills, leaving only a tiny contingent of older residents to ward off the Confederate assault. The small crew—numbering from three to 26, depending on the account—had only one little cannon and a great deal of ingenuity at their disposal. To make their numbers appear more impressive, the hilariously outnumbered brigade began lugging their sole piece of artillery from hilltop to hilltop, firing a shot and then rushing the weapon back down to give the illusion that the region was well-fortified.

The ruse didn't hold, however. When the bitter Confederates captured the cannon, they tossed it into the Missouri River before spending their brief occupation of Hermann like most tourists do—sampling the town's famous wine. The cannon, later fished from its watery grave, remains atop a hill at the Gasconade County Courthouse as an honored relic of an odd, bloodless fight.

The little cannon survived its big battle and even being thrown in the river, but its side blew open years later while being fired in celebration. The wound is still visible.

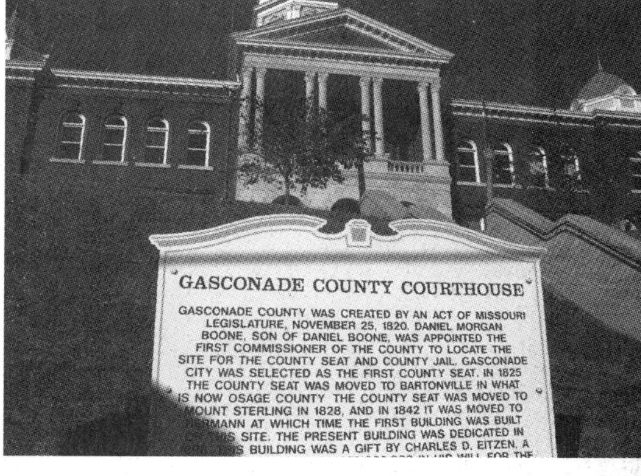

GASCONADE COUNTY COURTHOUSE
GASCONADE COUNTY WAS CREATED BY AN ACT OF MISSOURI LEGISLATURE, NOVEMBER 25, 1820. DANIEL MORGAN BOONE, SON OF DANIEL BOONE, WAS APPOINTED THE FIRST COMMISSIONER OF THE COUNTY TO LOCATE THE SITE FOR THE COUNTY SEAT AND COUNTY JAIL. GASCONADE CITY WAS SELECTED AS THE FIRST COUNTY SEAT. IN 1825 THE COUNTY SEAT WAS MOVED TO BARTONVILLE IN WHAT IS NOW OSAGE COUNTY. THE COUNTY SEAT WAS MOVED TO
STERLING IN 1828, AND IN 1842 IT WAS MOVED TO
AT WHICH TIME THE FIRST BUILDING WAS BUILT
SITE. THE PRESENT BUILDING WAS DEDICATED IN
BUILDING WAS A GIFT BY CHARLES D. EITZEN, A

While in Hermann, there is plenty to see and do. The Gasconade County Courthouse is thought to be the only courthouse in the nation constructed entirely with private dollars. Other attractions include the riverfront, the small-town antiques business, and, of course, the wineries.

5 DRAWING OUTSIDE THE LINES

Where can you travel from Missouri to Illinois without crossing a river?

When it comes to the bi-state area, the Mississippi River has become so strongly associated with our mutual border that it seems almost impossible to think of traversing from the Land of Lincoln to the Show Me State without going over a bridge.

Yet there are a few cartographic oddities between Kentucky and Iowa where you can indeed cross the Missouri–Illinois demarcation while remaining on dry land. One of these can be found east of West Alton, Missouri, near a fishing spot in front of the majestic Melvin Price Lock & Dam. About halfway down the gravel road, you'll officially enter the great state of Illinois, at a point where a portion of it protrudes rudely across the Mississippi.

Movement of the Mississippi after floods or earthquakes is not uncommon and has created various border deformations like this.

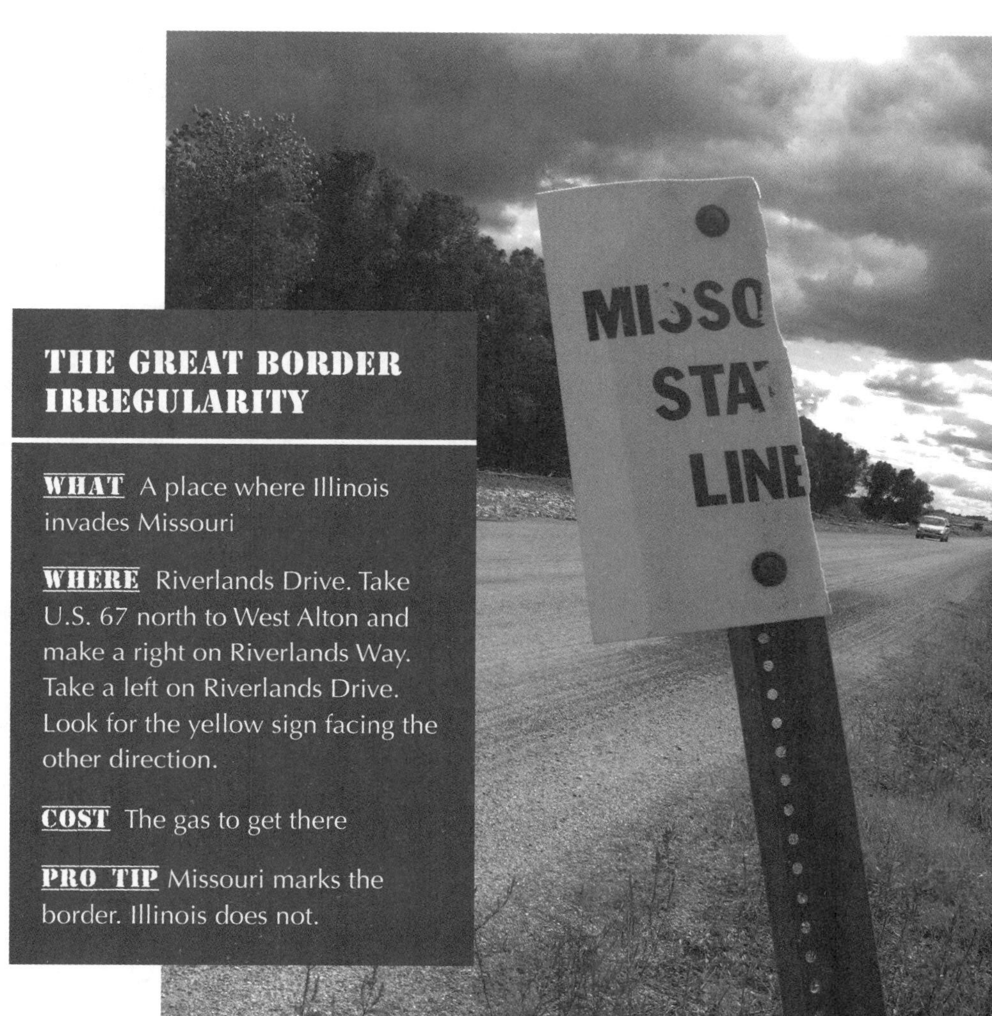

THE GREAT BORDER IRREGULARITY

WHAT A place where Illinois invades Missouri

WHERE Riverlands Drive. Take U.S. 67 north to West Alton and make a right on Riverlands Way. Take a left on Riverlands Drive. Look for the yellow sign facing the other direction.

COST The gas to get there

PRO TIP Missouri marks the border. Illinois does not.

This battered sign has seen better days, but it still marks a border few know about.

Unfortunately, no sign marks your crossing, but there is a small, yellow placard announcing your illustrious arrival back in Missouri. This means that an Illinoisan wishing to fish that part of the river would, if traveling by car, have to go through Missouri just to get to the desired part of his home state.

Incidentally, fishing licenses are accepted from authorities in both states at the location.

6 THE BROKEN HEART OF WEST COUNTY

Is Creve Coeur Lake really named after a famous suicide?

For most St. Louisans, Creve Coeur Lake is a favored place for a boating excursion or a relaxing jog, but its name is said to be rooted in a rather grisly urban legend. Meaning "broken heart" in French, the big pond's moniker supposedly derives from the tragic death of a Native American girl whose unrequited love caused her to leap from the Dripping Springs. A sign nearby commemorates the young lady's tragic demise.

While no one can know for sure, there is a very strong probability that the whole thing is just fanciful malarkey. Park signage can be a notoriously poor guide to history. Happily, however, the park does have a dark past. According to a St. Louis County history of the lake, it developed a seedy reputation for gin joints in the 1920s. "By the end of Prohibition," it notes, "Creve Coeur was almost exclusively a gangster hideout."

Most likely, the lake really takes its name from a number of locales in France or possibly its distinctive shape, which resembles half a heart. Incidentally, that shape is no accident. St. Louis County's most popular body of water is a so-called "ox-bow lake" that originally formed as a

---

Creve Coeur Lake used to have a smaller cousin called the "upper" lake but it vanished due to silt buildup.

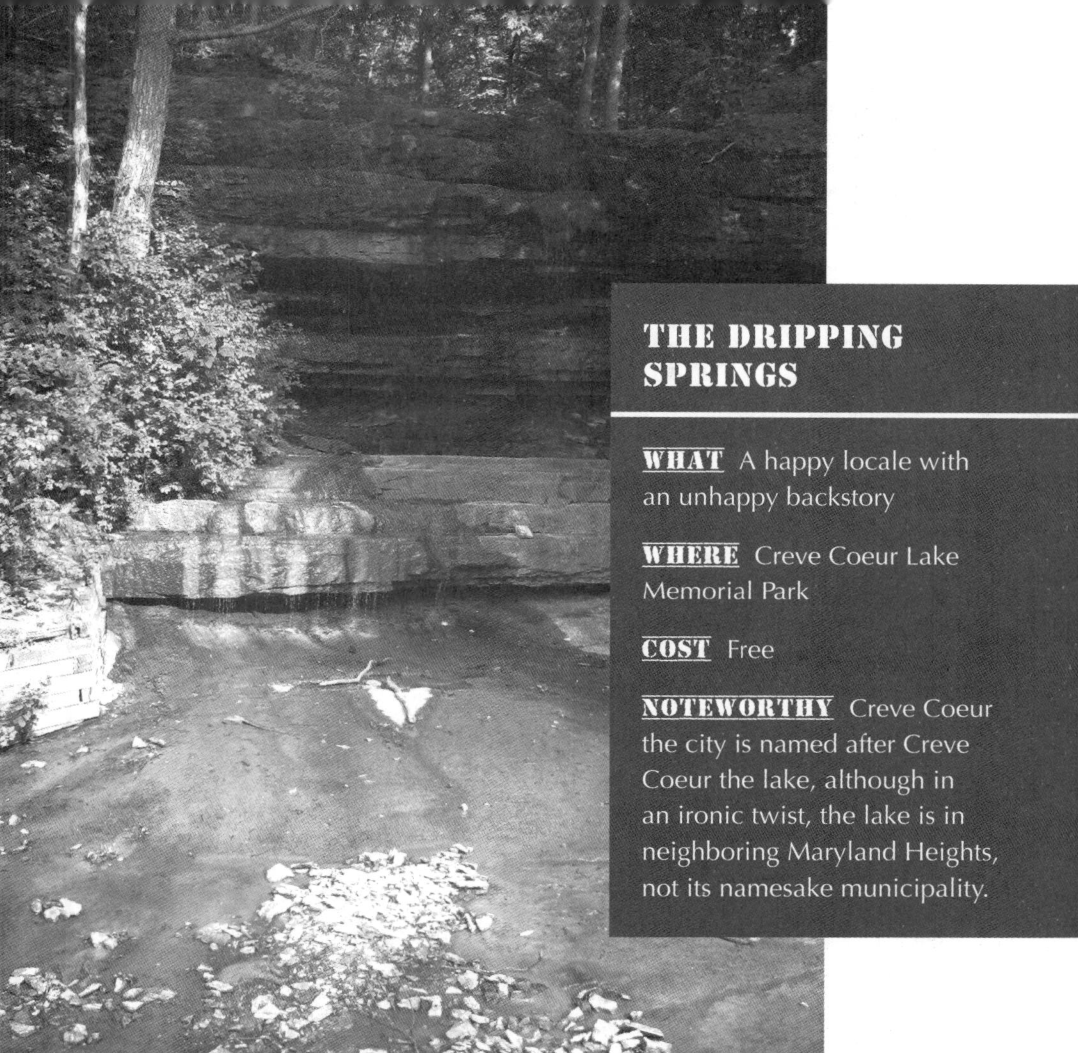

THE DRIPPING SPRINGS

WHAT A happy locale with an unhappy backstory

WHERE Creve Coeur Lake Memorial Park

COST Free

NOTEWORTHY Creve Coeur the city is named after Creve Coeur the lake, although in an ironic twist, the lake is in neighboring Maryland Heights, not its namesake municipality.

Despite dubious yarns of suicidal ladies and very real ones of gangsterism, the Dripping Springs are a pleasant stop for any traveler to Creve Coeur Lake Park.

now-abandoned bend in the nearby Missouri River when the latter cut a different course than it does today. Regardless of its genesis, this lake, now surrounded by the first county park, has become a family attraction, having outgrown its colorful past of spurned lovers and drunken ruffians. Today, it remains as a recreational treasure for local residents who desire an outdoorsy spot not too far from home.

7 THE STAIRCASE TO NOWHERE

Why is there a massive staircase leading to the Missouri River for no apparent reason?

With a presence as eerily deserted as it is bafflingly inexplicable, this mainstay of North County's Fort Belle Fontaine certainly lives up to its imposing billing as The Grand Staircase. Though what exactly the intricate stonework and grandiose grassy terraces of this beautifully ornate, richly detailed structure are doing perched on an unassuming river bluff has probably left more than a few visitors scratching their heads. It certainly wasn't part of the original fort, which graced the area from 1805 until 1826, and it seems to lead only to a nondescript riverbank and perfectly ordinary nature trail.

Actually, this impressive limestone treasure was a result of the Works Progress Administration, a Depression-era effort by the government to boost employment through large public infrastructure projects. Designed primarily to create paying positions for the able-bodied jobless, such projects were sometimes fashioned more to promote vocational vitality than fill any genuine need.

THE GRAND STAIRCASE

WHAT Stairs to nothing

WHERE Just keep heading north on Bellefontaine Road

COST Free

PRO TIP You'll have to sign in at the gate out front to access the area.

The Grand Staircase may not have a connection to the fort, but it remains a marvelous monument to the Depression-era industry of Franklin Delano Roosevelt's WPA.

Regardless, the Grand Staircase is a lovely stone masterwork, finely crafted by any standard. Only its lonely location seems out of place. Moreover, like any great deserted landmark, it is rumored to be haunted, with some claiming that a strange mist turns up from time to time in photos.

The 300-acre park itself is also worth a visit, with its network of nature trails and abundance of wildlife near the mouth of North County's Coldwater Creek.

The original Fort Belle Fontaine, the first U.S. military outpost west of the Mississippi, was essentially replaced by the modern-day Jefferson Barracks.

Meriwether Lewis and William Clark are among the notables to have camped at Fort Belle Fontaine during its heyday. The original site of the fort itself is now gone, having been washed away by a change in the course of the Missouri River, which it overlooked. But you can still explore the nature trails looping through trees near its remains.

8 AMERICAN GRAFFITI

Where can you go to experience a mile-long mural?

In any town near a waterway, a local floodwall might be merely a practicality borne of the river's wrath. But in St. Louis, the two miles of concrete paneling running beyond Chouteau Avenue do far more than just keep the area dry. It's become as much of a cultural touchstone as it is a feat of engineering.

Behold the St. Louis Graffiti Wall, an ever-changing monument to urban artistry that greets tourists who venture—or simply get lost—where the majestic downtown vistas of well-groomed Leonor K. Sullivan Boulevard transform into the disheveled, gritty scenescape of industrial Wharf Street.

As might befit an icon dedicated to an artform that is against the law in most other contexts, the city doesn't exactly put this strange taggers' haunt front and center in its promotional materials. In fact, Paint Louis, the annual event that began inviting artists from around the nation to muralize the wall in the late 1990s, has had a sometimes uneasy relationship with the local authorities, who ultimately cancelled the initiative when a few rogue participants were unable to confine their creative enthusiasm to the legally allowed concrete canvas. In recent years, however, the gathering has reemerged, and the wall's proud tradition as an impromptu venue for aesthetic elan has continued.

The heavily tagged viaduct beneath Tower Grove and Vandeventer is called "The Arena" by graffiti artists who paint there.

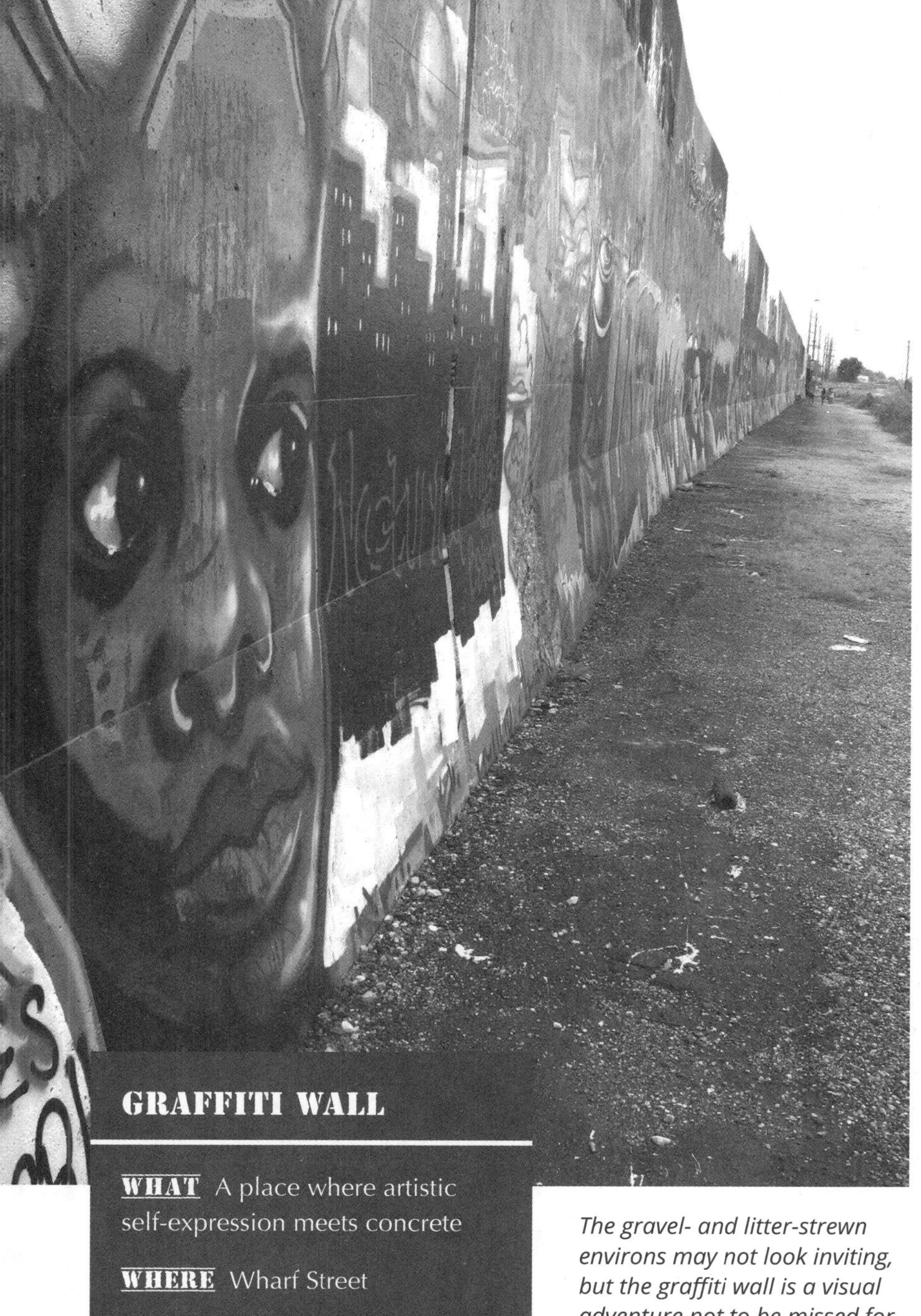

GRAFFITI WALL

WHAT A place where artistic self-expression meets concrete

WHERE Wharf Street

COST Free

PRO TIP Bring a camera and take a stroll or just tour in the car.

The gravel- and litter-strewn environs may not look inviting, but the graffiti wall is a visual adventure not to be missed for any true patron of street art.

9 ESCAPE FROM MISSOURI

What role did the Chain of Rocks Bridge play in a cinematic classic?

Speaking of a bridge over troubled waters may seem a cliché, but for the old Chain of Rocks span, constructed over an extremely hazardous section of river ultimately bypassed by the canal of the same name, it is all too true. Even the bridge's design, with its bizarre bend at midstream, reveals a difficult history that goes all the way back to the beginning, when complaints from those navigating the river—as well as structural issues anchoring to the Missouri side—necessitated the span's odd mid-river twist. In later years, financial woes plagued the bridge. Opened in 1929, it ultimately shut down in 1968, its fate sealed by completion of the nearby interstate crossing. The only reason Chain of Rocks wasn't torn down the following decade was because doing so would have cost too much. In 1991, the deserted bridge even gained local infamy as the site of a horrifying, high-profile double murder.

However, not all of Chain of Rocks' history was so tragic. The dilapidated connector's gritty past and abandoned present were precisely what director John Carpenter was looking for when he was filming the post-apocalyptic thrillride *Escape from New York*, a 1981 flick that re-envisioned the Big Apple as a huge futuristic mega-prison. As a stand-in for the heavily

---

St. Louis's Union Station was a stand-in for Grand Central Station in *Escape from New York*.

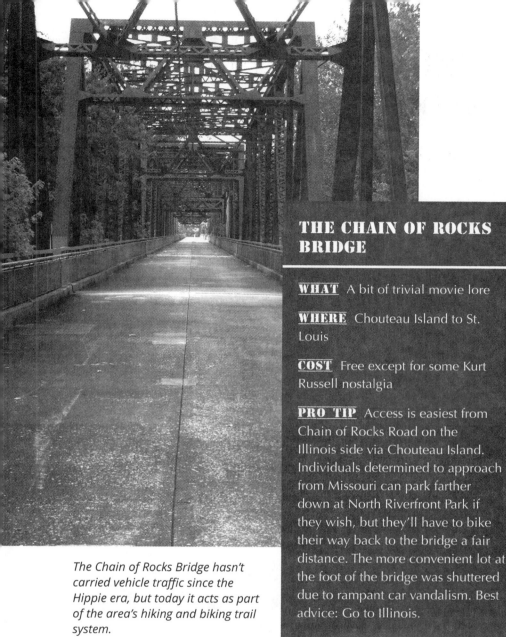

The Chain of Rocks Bridge hasn't carried vehicle traffic since the Hippie era, but today it acts as part of the area's hiking and biking trail system.

THE CHAIN OF ROCKS BRIDGE

WHAT A bit of trivial movie lore

WHERE Chouteau Island to St. Louis

COST Free except for some Kurt Russell nostalgia

PRO TIP Access is easiest from Chain of Rocks Road on the Illinois side via Chouteau Island. Individuals determined to approach from Missouri can park farther down at North Riverfront Park if they wish, but they'll have to bike their way back to the bridge a fair distance. The more convenient lot at the foot of the bridge was shuttered due to rampant car vandalism. Best advice: Go to Illinois.

mined 69th Street Bridge in the movie's climatic scene, the Chain of Rocks became immortalized as part of the history of what would later become a true cult classic.

10 PICNIC AT THE TOXIC WASTE DUMP

What is that strange mountain of rocks off of Route 94?

Rising incongruously some 75 feet above the surrounding St. Charles County countryside, this huge 45-acre mountain of limestone in Weldon Spring provides such a breathtaking vista that it is said you can even see the Gateway Arch more than 30 miles away on a clear day. But this gigantic manmade behemoth of stones wasn't constructed just for your viewing pleasure, nor even for easy access to local nature trails. In fact, it was made to contain something else that man made—and now wishes very much he could get rid of.

This oddly unnatural rocky mesa is actually a toxic waste disposal cell. Once you trudge up the stairs, you are standing atop nearly one-and-a-half million cubic yards of truly undesirable materials. Much of it is chemical residue from conventional weapons programs the military ran in the area during WWII, but some of the entombed refuse is radioactive leftovers from uranium production programs. Don't expect the mountain to be taken away anytime soon. Some of the thorium stored in the site has an impressive half-life of 14

WELDON SPRING DISPOSAL CELL

WHAT 1.48 million cubic yards of toxic waste with an awesome view

WHERE 7295 Highway 94 South

COST Free

PRO TIP No need to arrive early. Crowds are rare.

Covering 45 acres, this huge pile of stones was specially constructed to contain both nuclear and conventional wastes used in weapons production.

billion years, somewhat older than the age of the planet, so this remediation isn't exactly a short-term project. Officials say there is no reason for concern, however, and in fact, you will get less radioactive exposure at the top of the cell than in your own backyard. There's even a picnic table nearby in case you want to pack a lunch and take your midday meal at the base of the toxic mountain. Also, be sure to visit the interpretive center, where friendly staff and informative exhibits will explain precisely what's trapped in the cell, how extremely harmful it is, and how—thankfully—it can't get out and do terrible things to you.

As huge as it is, the site is actually only a fraction of the more than 17,000-acre chunk of St. Charles County the military claimed under a state of emergency during WWII. Today, a significant portion of the land makes up the pleasant, lake-strewn August A. Busch Wildlife Area.

Three entire towns were leveled when the military assumed control of the area in WWII.

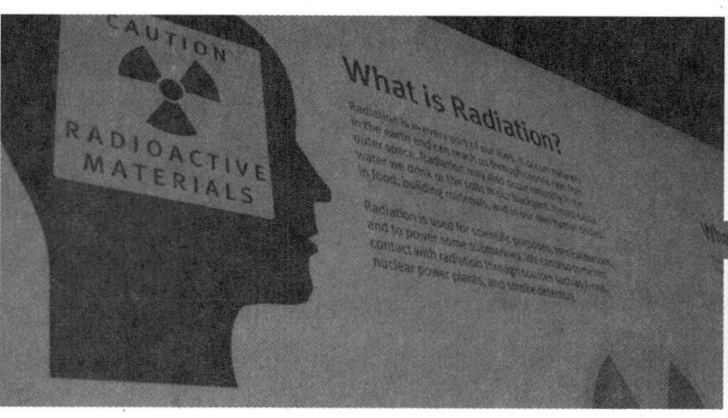

The Weldon Spring site is far more than just a disposal cell for hazardous materials. The on-site interpretive center contains a wealth of information and exhibits related to radiation and military operations in the area and a tribute to the uranium plant workers employed in Weldon Spring from 1957–66, as well as a facility in St. Louis earlier during WWII.

11 THE REAL HOME OF REAL ROCK RADIO

Did St. Louis's KSHE 95 start in the basement of a Crestwood house?

Radio station KSHE 95 has long been a St. Louis institution. But few know that "the home of real rock radio" opened its broadcasting life in a real home. It went on the air from the Crestwood residence of a fellow by the name of Rudolph Ceries, who took the concept of underground radio literally. The studio was in his basement. According to the St. Louis Media History Foundation, Ceries's wife used to press her husband's shirts in the makeshift records library, and the news department consisted of wire service dispatches printing out next to the washing machine. Some of the equipment used for the nascent station was homemade.

Sweetmeat, the famous pig logo,was named in 1974 by an Affton 11th grader, who won 50 pounds of bacon for the idea.

KSHE'S FIRST LOCATION

WHAT A home for the home of real rock radio

WHERE 1035 Westglen

COST None

PRO TIP There are no tours. This is not a public facility. It is a private residence where people actually live. Do not bother them.

This unassuming Crestwood abode was where one of the Gateway area's most well-known radio enterprises got its humble start.

Incidentally, while modern listeners might recognize the iconic station's call letters, when it took to the airwaves in 1961 they certainly would have found the format unfamiliar. Ceries's tastes ran less to hard-driving rock and more to light classical selections.

He also took advantage of the station's call letters, branding it "the lady" of FM radio and even employing females as the voice of KSHE.

KSHE's days as Ceries's little rec room project were numbered, however. Three years after it began, it was under new management. Classical selections had already begun to dwindle in favor of the newly emerging rock genre that was fast sweeping the nation. Today, the station is owned by Emmis Communications and has long since moved out of the basement.

12 MOUND AT THE MUSIAL

What's that large rock doing at the end of Mound Street?

Mound Street isn't much to look at—a truncated stub of pavement a few hundred feet long coming off an unremarkable stretch of North Broadway. However, its name holds the key to its specialness—as does the big pink boulder that lies near its dead end.

The pre-Columbian earthen hills that give St. Louis its Mound City nickname were no natural feature, and they once dominated both sides of the river. At Cahokia in Illinois, they can still be seen, but the mound-building culture's works on the St. Louis side of the river were ultimately destroyed.

BIG MOUND

WHAT A gravestone for a piece of irreplaceable history

WHERE Mound Street off North Broadway

COST Free

NOTEWORTHY The only remaining native earthwork in the City of St. Louis is Sugarloaf Mound on Ohio Street. It is now privately owned by a local tribe.

"Cahokia" wasn't really what the mound-builders were called. It was the name of a later tribe living here when the French arrived.

This rock pays sad tribute to the loss of Big Mound, one of many native structures destroyed by the city's expansion.

That was also the unfortunate fate of Big Mound, a structure some 30 feet high north of downtown that afforded a commanding view of both the river and the bustling city developing alongside it. Regrettably, just after the Civil War, that development would consume the mound itself along with many others in the same area. A stone bearing a plaque in the shadow of the Stan Musial Bridge is the only remaining testimony to mourn the loss of Big Mound.

It wasn't alone. Missouri's impressive collection of mounds was decimated as the population spread. Sixteen of the structures were leveled in Forest Park just to make room for the Louisiana Purchase Exposition of 1904.

Today, little evidence remains of the once-great metropolis that predated our present city.

13 A DIAMOND IN THE ROUGH

Is there a place in St. Louis where you can drive on the "wrong" side of the road?

It is easy to notice something just a bit weird about the intersection of Dorsett Road and Interstate 270. As Dorsett motorists move beneath the overpass, they skew across the oncoming lanes and suddenly find themselves in a situation deeply unfamiliar to most American drivers—operating a vehicle on the left side of the road! As they exit the overpass, the drivers reverse places again and traffic returns to its usual flow pattern.

Welcome to the "diverging diamond" interchange in Maryland Heights, a traffic management system so unique that it was only the fourth example to be opened in the nation when it was created in late 2010. As of 2015, the Dorsett/I-270 overpass was still one of only about 50 in the country. The diverging diamond is thought to simplify high-capacity intersections by avoiding waits for left turns that would normally bottle up cars wishing to enter the highway onramp. Instead, drivers can glide to the left without crossing opposing traffic. The design, while still rare, is now operational in states from New York to Nevada. In 2013, the I-70 interchange at Mid Rivers Mall Drive became the only other in the area where St. Louis motorists can experience driving on the "wrong" side of the road.

Maryland Heights was given its moniker by settlers from the state of that name.

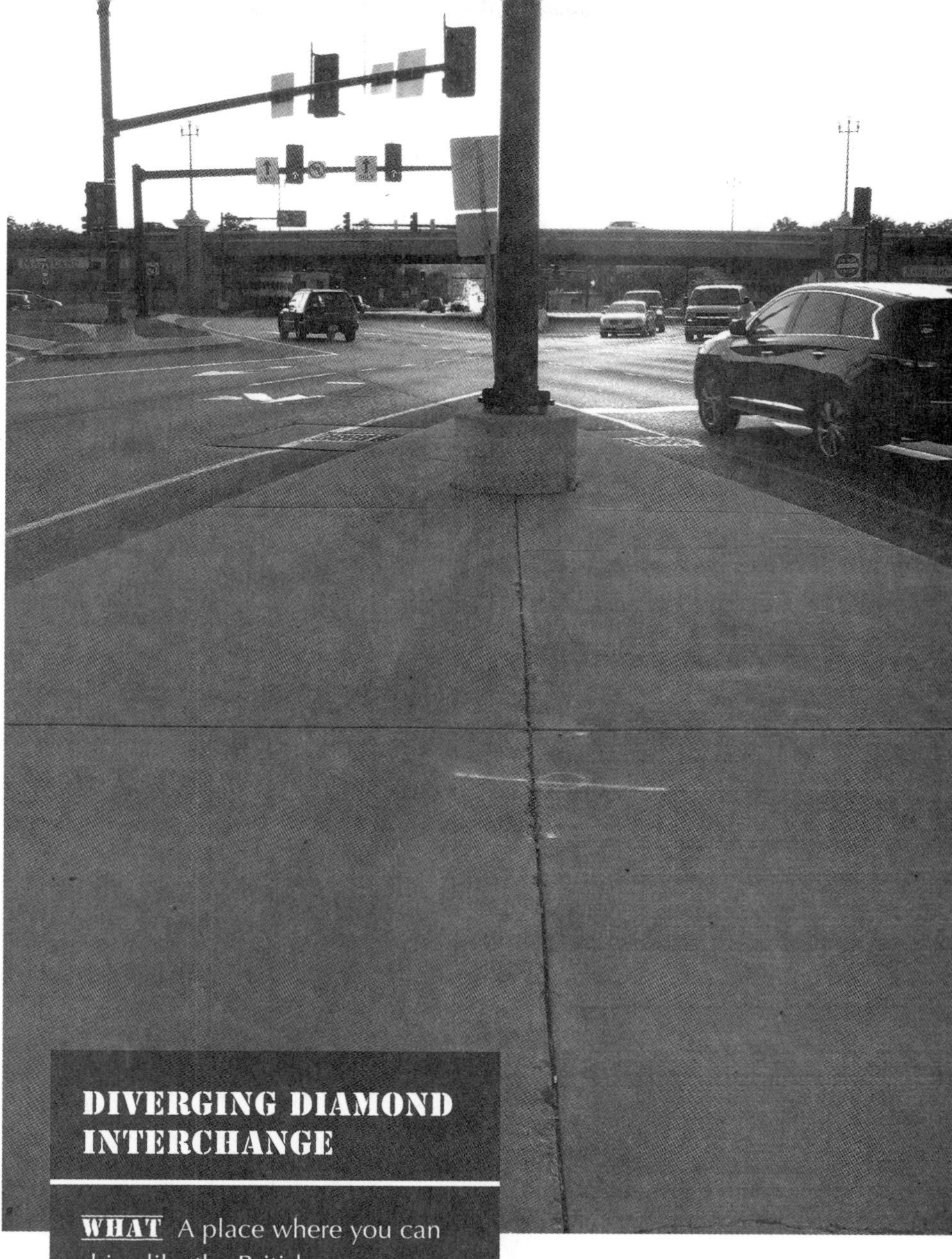

DIVERGING DIAMOND INTERCHANGE

WHAT A place where you can drive like the British

WHERE I-270 and Dorsett Road

COST Free

NOTEWORTHY Three of the first four U.S. diverging diamond interchanges were in Missouri.

Opened in 2010, this "diverging diamond" interchange made St. Louis a national pioneer in traffic management systems.

14 THE BATTLE OF ST. LOUIS

Was a Revolutionary War battle once fought in downtown?

Okay, so it won't rank up there with Lexington, Concord, or Bunker Hill but, unknown to many, St. Louis does have a Revolutionary War claim to fame. In 1780, downtown St. Louis was the site of the Battle of San Carlos, the westernmost battle fought in America's war for independence.

Oddly, as the marvelous *Distilled History* blog points out, this campaign of the American Revolution is unique for having had a distinct lack of actual Americans. There were virtually no representatives of the United States in the battle. Instead, it was a fight between a British force made up mostly of Fox and Sauk Indians and a Spanish force composed

---

FORT SAN CARLOS

WHAT The sole battle of the American revolution to be fought west of the Mississippi

WHERE Walnut Street and Broadway

COST Free

PRO TIP According to *Distilled History*, the plaque lauding the battle is probably about a block west of the real site of the tower.

Regarded badly by St. Louisans, the victorious but unpopular Spanish commander Fernando de Leyba died roughly a month after the battle he won.

primarily of Frenchmen and slaves. The British, hoping to gain a foothold in the West along the river, were the aggressors. The defending Spanish forces mostly protected a large trench they'd dug centered on what would eventually become the Gateway Arch grounds, fortified by a small stone tower at what is now Walnut Street. According to *Distilled History*, the current site of Busch Stadium would have afforded a fine view of the British assault from the north.

The attackers were ultimately repulsed, leaving about 25 dead between both combatants. The only evidence of their efforts today is a commemorative plaque in front of the Hilton St. Louis at the Ballpark, which most hotel guests probably walk by without giving much thought to the blood spilled there.

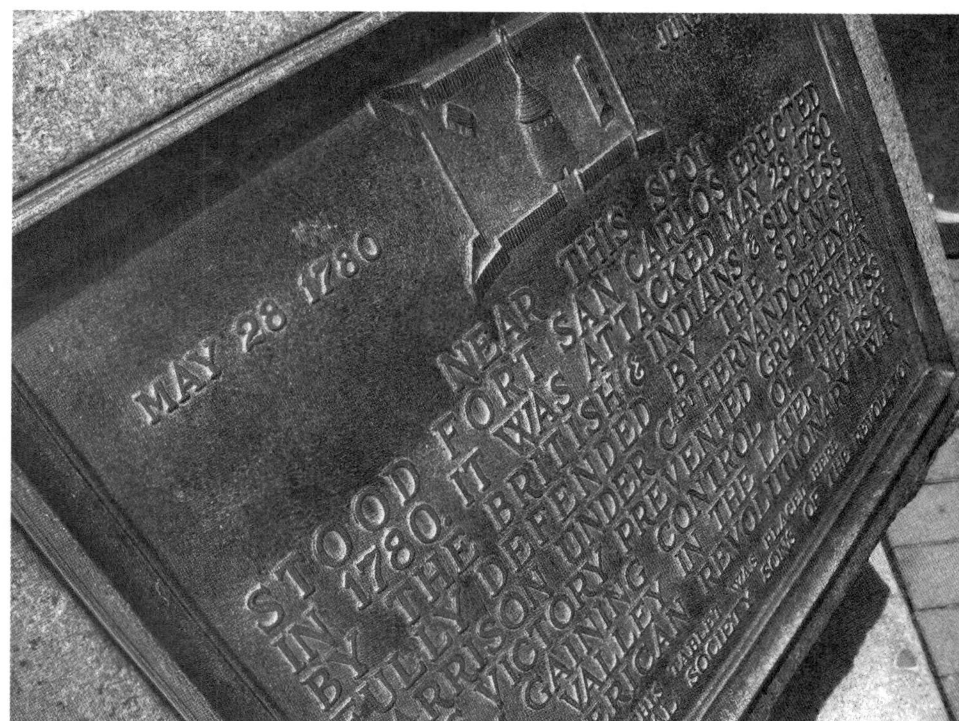

George Washington may not have slept here but we St. Louisans do indeed have our own piece of the American Revolution.

15 NEVER AGAIN

Where can you find St. Louis's Genocide Clock?

There are some solemn tasks that humanity wishes weren't necessary. Chronicling each of the staggering 111 million estimated victims of genocide since WWII is certainly one of them. But this vital work is being done right here in the Gateway City. Every 19 seconds, another number is added to the total on the Genocide Clock at St. Louis's own Holocaust Museum and Learning Center in Memory of Gloria M. Goldstein (HMLC) to memorialize another victim of the mass killings that continue to plague our world.

Holocaust museums are uncommon in the Midwest, and the HMLC remains a remarkable educational resource for information regarding one of history's most tragic eras. With multimedia exhibits, interactive displays, and a collection of original documents and artifacts from Holocaust survivors who settled in St. Louis, the HMLC displays everything from Nazi propaganda posters to travel papers to the typical uniform worn by those interned at a concentration camp. By its very nature, much of the material in the facility is raw, emotional, and disquieting, but the institution communicates

HOLOCAUST MUSEUM AND LEARNING CENTER

WHAT A clock that reminds us that inhumanity still exists

WHERE 12 Millstone Campus Drive

COST Free (donations accepted)

NOTEWORTHY The HMLC is closed on Saturday.

On average, every 19 seconds another person falls victim to the scourge of genocide somewhere on the planet—a sad tally being chronicled right here in St. Louis.

a vital message important for all ages. In fact, schools from around the area regularly sponsor field trips to the museum. Some of the most disturbing imagery is kept behind a partition and can be viewed at the visitor's discretion.

The HMLC also goes beyond the history of the Holocaust itself by regularly doing anti-bias work to combat hatred, bigotry, and violations of human rights through projects such as the Genocide Clock, which reminds viewers that the promise of "never again" made after the death camps were liberated has not been forgotten—but unfortunately, neither has it been fulfilled.

In 1939, a ship with more than 900 Jewish refugees escaping Hitler's wrath was denied entry to the U.S. and forced to return to Europe. Its name became imfamous as a symbol of how little other nations did to take in those in need. It was called the *St. Louis*.

Many of the exhibits at the HMLC tell the personal stories of individual survivors who later settled to start new lives and raise families in the St. Louis area. Others focus more broadly on one of human history's most brutal atrocities by highlighting aspects of life for Jews and others caught in the tightening Nazi noose.

16 PEACE, LOVE, AND . . . BARGAINS

Why does a dove represent a Des Peres mall?

An iconic symbol for generations of I-270 travelers, the famous dove insignia has flown high above West County Center for decades, becoming as closely associated with the mall as tasteful eateries and fashionable clothiers.

But more than a few might have questioned how this big white avian, long a sign of the counterculture, came to hover over one of the area's busiest centers of commerce.

According to *Under the Dove*, a 2002 book inspired by the design, the answer lies with a fellow named Joe Thaler, the art designer tasked with coming up with a logo for a new mall about to open in then-sparsely populated West County. It may also lie with the time in which he was doing it—1968. A young man with a good corporate job, Thaler felt he had "one foot in each camp" when it came to the cultural fault line then splitting the nation.

Thaler's eventual choice was the pole-mounted symbol we see today. Though he initially considered a number of animal designs—including an eagle and even a dragon—Thaler eventually gravitated toward a bird shape, which he found graceful and non-threatening. Surprisingly, he didn't

---

Though only 64 feet tall at its creation, the dove's pole now holds it aloft at 83 feet.

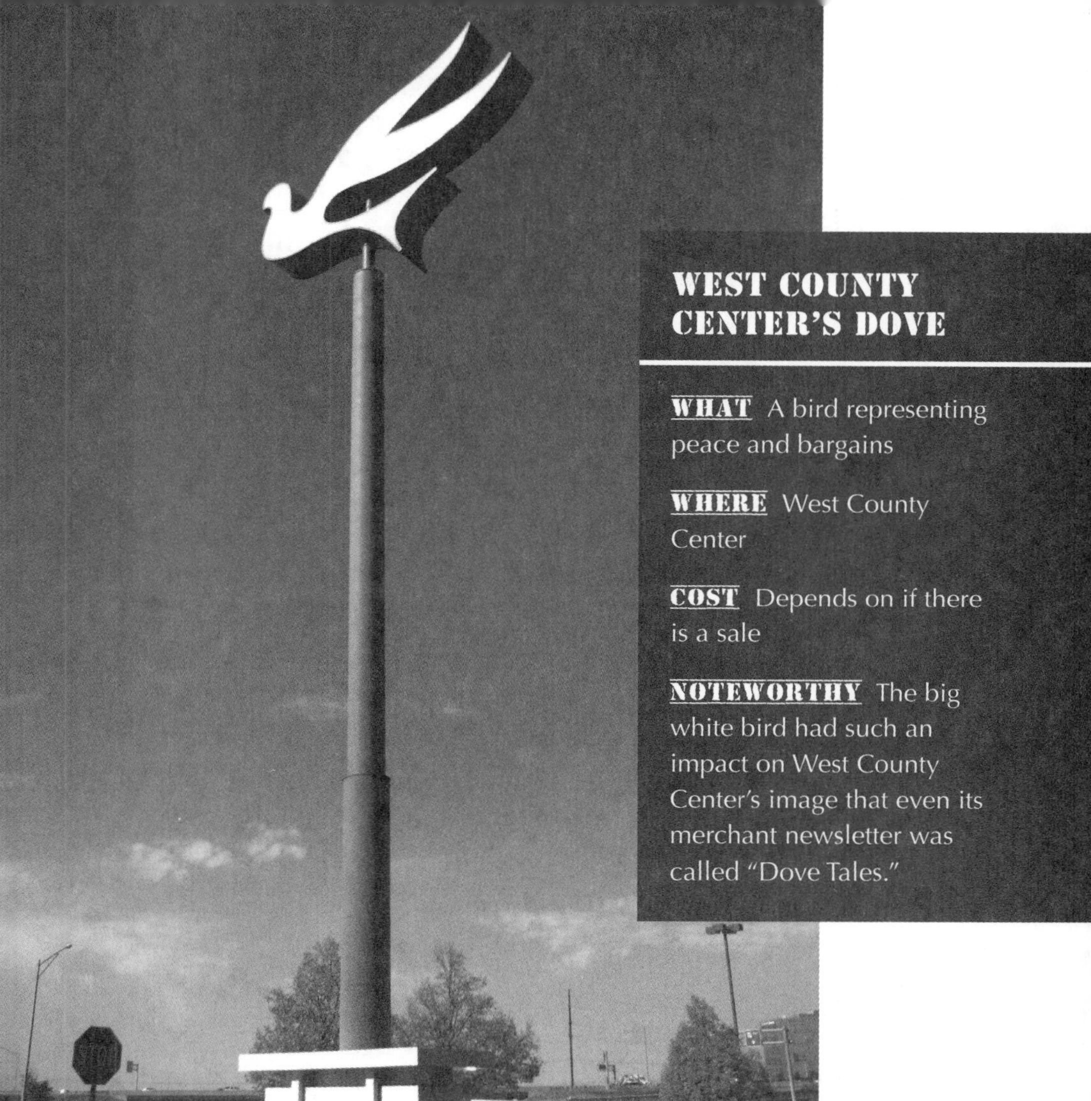

WEST COUNTY CENTER'S DOVE

WHAT A bird representing peace and bargains

WHERE West County Center

COST Depends on if there is a sale

NOTEWORTHY The big white bird had such an impact on West County Center's image that even its merchant newsletter was called "Dove Tales."

This famous St. Louis symbol is still flying high after all these years. To think that it could have been a dragon.

even envision the form as being explicitly a dove but rather a more generic avian outline. "I didn't really think about what kind of bird it was," he said.

But when they saw it, people begin identifying it as the famous Biblical symbol of peace. And the rest is history.

17 HALF A HIGHWAY

Why does I-170 end in the middle of a shopping center?

St. Louis has a fine highway system. Interstate 55 rolls in from the south before heading in a Chicago-ly direction. I-64 bisects the metro area into neat halves and then wanders to the East Coast. Interstates 70 and 44 shoot in from the northwest and southwest, respectively, while I-270 and 255 loop the area nicely.

Then there is poor old Interstate 170, the sadly truncated "innerbelt" that clearly belts nothing, running nearly due south for its 13-mile length before leading motorists, rather unceremoniously, to the wall of a local department store.

Any quick glance at a map will show the problem. While the rest of the system seems logically laid out, our north/south expressway seems to have forgotten the "south" part, stopping dead in mid-county and leaving commuters to jog east to a congested Hanley Road or continue straight

I-170 TERMINUS

WHAT The broken dreams of traffic planners

WHERE The lovely shops of the Brentwood Promenade

COST None

PRO TIP In lieu of the nonexistent interstate, Metro trains can provide a convenient conveyance southward from Brentwood to the Shrewsbury station.

Much of I-270 was designated as Interstate 244 until the 1970s.

As every motorist knows, there is only one way to go from Eager Road.

into a parking lot for bargain hunting at the fashionable Brentwood Promenade shopping complex. So why is there no highway farther south than the wilds of Richmond Heights?

The short answer is that there was supposed to be. The roots of Interstate 170 lay initially in a mid-county route designated 725 that was built decades ago in anticipation of a true north/south connector. That vision seemed to emerge with the extension of the highway farther north to I-270 in the 1980s, at which time it earned its interstate designation.

However, residents and businesses protested and killed a planned expansion to the south the following decade, leaving the highway permanently shortened, its abrupt terminus nothing more than a boon for Target and Trader Joe's.

18 SMALLPOX ISLAND

Where can you pay respects to a tragic piece of Civil War history?

The horrors inflicted by the Civil War have been well-documented for generations by Americans through history books and family lore alike. Wounds inflicted by the era's rifle technology could be brutal. A lingering death for those left on the field or a gruesome amputation for those taken from it were not uncommon during the conflict.

But some of the worst suffering may have been seen by prisoners of war who were all-too-often mistreated, starved, neglected, or left to the ravages of disease. The last of these was the fate of dozens of Confederate prisoners of war held at the overcrowded and undersupplied federal POW camp in Alton.

The Alton prison lives on even today. Stones from the infamous institution, which shut down in 1865, are said to have been found in numerous other walls around the Illinois city.

SMALLPOX ISLAND MARKER

WHAT Where disease claimed lives the battlefield did not

WHERE The Lincoln-Shields Recreation Area near West Alton

COST Free

PRO TIP A cemetery for the Confederate dead from the larger Alton prison can also be found at 635 Rozier Street, where a massive plinth memorializes the otherwise unmarked graves.

The memorial for the Confederate dead from Smallpox Island remains near the site of the old Lock and Dam No. 26, the construction of which uncovered some of the prisoners' remains.

When, in 1862, an epidemic eventually broke out, many perished, most of them housed at a makeshift quarantine facility on a strip of land in the Mississippi initially called Sunflower Island. Today, it is colloquially known to history by the much less cheerful sobriquet "Smallpox Island."

The marker memorializing the dead isn't on the exact location of the island itself, which was later reclaimed by the Mississippi. Instead it sits in the Lincoln-Shields Recreation Area on the Missouri side of the river. Even the location of the Confederate remains were lost to history until decades later when their unmarked graves were unearthed during an engineering project.

Some of the dead are said to still lie beneath the water near the regulation pool of today's Melvin Price Locks and Dam.

19 THE GHOSTS OF TIMES BEACH

What sad secret lies beneath a Southwest County park?

Nestled into a bend of the scenic Meramec River, visitors will find few things lovelier than Route 66 State Park. Walking and horse-riding trails crisscross a landscape of native grasses. On any given day, wildlife scampers about and picnickers can enjoy the seasonable warmth of a summer's afternoon.

But this bucolic locale has a history and the secret which lies beneath it reveals the tragic truth that this beautiful park should never have existed at all.

A town died here and this lovely bit of green space is its unmarked grave.

The community in question was Times Beach, a municipality of a few hundred that disappeared from

---

ROUTE 66 STATE PARK

WHAT A buried town

WHERE Interstate 44 at the Williams Road exit

COST Free unless you get hooked by something in the really endearing gift shop

PRO TIP Make a point of stopping by the visitor's center, which has a marvelous museum.

Times Beach acquired its name from the St. Louis Times newspaper, which distributed lots to boost subscriptions.

maps in 1985 after being accidentally contaminated with dioxin, a toxic chemical that was dumped in waste oil upon the roads to keep down dust. When the contamination became known, Times Beach became a story from coast to coast. Forced to evacuate, its residents were bought out and the town demolished to make way for a dioxin incinerator that finished its work by the late 1990s.

The visitors' center for the park, which is now considered safe by the EPA, still houses artifacts from the now-deceased municipality, which briefly became a national household word for toxic accidents. The demolished remains of the city's structures are interred beneath the park which remains a silent warning of the dangers of being too careless with the chemicals man's genius has allowed him to create.

Beneath this park lies the town of Times Beach, a victim of 20th-century carelessness and a sad lesson in caution for future generations.

20 THE GHOSTS OF TIMES BEACH, PT. 2

Why is this park separated from its own visitors' center by a strange bridge with no road?

The sign near the visitor's center is friendly enough. "You are always welcome in Missouri State Parks," it reads. But just a few yards ahead are the "Stop" and "Road closed" signs. That's because the bridge, which connects the visitor's center to its park, no longer has a roadbed.

Yet this hulk isn't slated for demolition. In fact, it is the centerpiece of Route 66 State Park. The iconic highway of that name ran through here after the bridge's construction, which was completed the same year FDR was elected to his first term in the White House. Its unique "Warren Truss"

Supporters hope that someday this bridge will once again carry traffic as it did when it was still part of America's most famous highway.

ROUTE 66 STATE PARK VISITORS CENTER

WHAT A bridge you cannot cross

WHERE Take Interstate 44 to the Lewis Road exit and take the N. Outer Road west

COST Free

NOTEWORTHY Route 66 was first designated in 1926.

structure is one of the few of that type in the state.

By 2009, however, the span, which is on the National Register of Historic Places, had become too deteriorated to carry traffic. Today, it sits silently awaiting funding so it can carry cars again.

It would also connect the park to its own visitor's center, which now requires a ludicrously tortuous four-mile trek of double-backs and exit ramps to travel a few hundred yards as the crow flies.

But don't let the journey discourage you. The center, a treasure trove of Route 66 memorabilia and souvenirs, is well worth a visit.

The roadless bridge above the Meramec measures just over 1,000 feet long.

Route 66 comes to life in the visitor's center museum and gift shop. From old road signage to Coral Court Motel ephemera, this institution tells the story of America's most famous pre-interstate strip of pavement. Special sections also commemorate the tragedy of Times Beach.

21 THE NATIONAL'S FIRST NO-NO

Was the no-hitter invented in St. Louis?

As one of pitching's most illustrious achievements, the no-hitter remains the crowning glory for any hurler's career. Yet most don't know that the first recorded no-hit game in either currently existing major league was inked into the books right here in St. Louis.

That's where, on July 15, 1876, George Bradley of the St. Louis Browns retired 27 Hartford Dark Blues without giving up a single base knock. The 2-0 win was the first no-hitter posted in the newly formed National League. Bradley would go on to win 45 games that year with a

ALL-STAR FIELD

WHAT A piece of baseball history

WHERE The Herbert Hoover Boys & Girls Club at 2901 North Grand Avenue

COST Free

NOTEWORTHY The city's first Busch Stadium wasn't downtown. It was here. In its later years, the venerable Sportsman's Park took on the brewery's name before the former's eventual demolition, so officially, there have been three Busch Stadiums, not two.

Taking someone out to the old ballgame was easy enough at this legendary North-side site, where the greats of the game plied their trade.

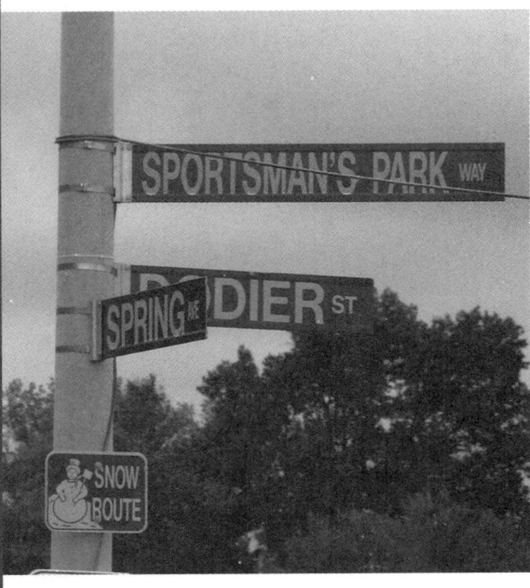

career-best 1.23 ERA. His no-hitter was part of a 37-inning scoreless streak he put together that saw him nearly no-hit Cincinnati days later.

The site where Bradley made his mark was known as the Grand Avenue Ball Grounds, a plot of land at Grand and Dodier Street that would later contain Sportsman's Park.

Fittingly, the spot is still a haven for America's favorite pastime, serving as a ballfield for the Herbert Hoover Boys & Girls Club.

According to ProjectBallpark.org, "Baseball was played on this site longer than anywhere else in the world."

Today, the St. Louis Browns still exist—as the modern Baltimore Orioles.

If baseball is St. Louis's unofficial religion, then this unassuming chunk of real estate qualifies as its longest-running church. Now called All-Star Field, this site has played host to various ballparks since just after the Civil War.

Once home to two baseball teams, the park lost the first in 1953 with the departure of the St. Louis Browns to the East Coast. Major League baseball ended here completely in 1966 with the construction of a new stadium downtown for the Cardinals. Yet it remains forever a key part of the city's rich athletic heritage.

22 A RIVER DOESN'T RUN THROUGH IT

Why is Des Peres named for a waterway nowhere near it?

Des Peres has long been known as a charming residential locale in West County. Yet, more than once, its curious label must have provoked a question or two. Clearly, it is named after the River Des Peres, but how exactly did a suburb straddling Interstate 270 get tagged with the moniker of a waterway that rings the southern border of the City of St. Louis, a solid 20-minute trek down Manchester Road? The river never comes closer than seven miles or so to the town.

The answer can be found in the foggy mists of the River Des Peres' history. Meaning "River of the Fathers," it was named for Jesuit priests who briefly resided near its mouth in the early 1700s. Later, 19th-century adventurers into

---

Des Peres's stately city hall was once a Depression-era home for orphans.

DES PERES

WHAT A town named for what it doesn't possess

WHERE If you are at Manchester and I-270, you're there

COST None

NOTEWORTHY Des Peres has a population of more than 8,300 residents, according to the 2010 census.

This affluent suburb has a wealth of creeks and streams, but when it comes to the "River of the Fathers," the City of Des Peres remains miles away from its hydrological parent.

the backwoods of the still-undeveloped St. Louis County followed the river to one of its western branches near Maplewood called Deer Creek, which in turn has its own tributary system, including tiny Two Mile Creek, which happens to run through modern day Des Peres.

Of course, rivers don't come equipped with convenient signage, so there was a tendency to simply refer to whatever stream you were following as whatever creek you just left. The whole area just sort of became "Des Peres," a name that was in use at least a century before the town itself was organized in 1934.

23 MIRRORED MAPLEWOOD

Why is the word Maplewood seen in reverse on the opposite side of a Metro overpass?

No, this wasn't an error by tired workmen. The bridge that conveys Metro tracks across Manchester Road does indeed have the word "Maplewood" on both sides—and the rendering on the east side is very much in reverse.

The lettering, which is backlit at night, is a work of art, and the effect is quite intentional. It is all about creative license. Janet Zweig, an award-winning Brooklyn, N.Y., artist who fashioned the piece out of debris derived from local homes that were torn down, intends viewers to see Maplewood both coming and going. Those entering the

---

THE BACKWARDS MAPLEWOOD

WHAT A message meant for a mirror

WHERE 7845 Manchester Road

COST Free (or eerF if you are heading west)

PRO TIP Tough to stop and see this one. The Metro station doesn't provide parking. You'll have to enjoy it while driving.

Maplewood derives its name from the type of tree planted by the subdivision's original planners.

city motoring east on Manchester will see the letters on the west side. If they look in their mirrors and see the east side of the overpass, they will still see a forward-facing Maplewood, since the lettering is flipped. According to the city's website, the idea is to create "an illusionistic image of Maplewood's past" in your rear view mirror. Pretty clever, eh?

So, what about westbound drivers?

Well, they'll just be a little confused—but hey, they are leaving town anyway, so why worry?

How did a forward-thinking town end up with backward-looking signage? It is just the creative mind at work. Like Maplewood's storied past, the lettering is meant to be seen in the rearview mirror.

24 STROLLIN' ZOMBIE ROAD

Are there really otherworldly forces at work in West County?

Let's get something straight: its real name is Lawler Ford Road, although these days it is known as the Rock Hollow Trail. Regardless, no organ of government ever gave this much-maligned 2.3-mile path across Wildwood the chill-inducing sobriquet bestowed upon it by a generation of illicit nocturnal West County tourists. Nonetheless, most St. Louisans will forever know it as Zombie Road.

The trail, once a Civil War-era route to Jefferson County which became a gravel-hauling road from the banks of the Meramec River, has in more recent years become a haunt for paranormal enthusiasts and teenagers looking to scare themselves silly with a midnight sojourn to what most people agree is among the creepiest wooded spots in the area. Those who have made the pilgrimage have reported everything from "shadow people" lurking about to strange voices and

ROCK HOLLOW TRAIL

WHAT: A path with a ghostly reputation

WHERE: Trailhead is at Ridge Meadows Elementary School, 777 Ridge Road

COST: Free and fun by day (expensive and illegal by night)

PRO TIP: Parking is available during school hours.

The daytime beauty of the heavily wooded Rock Hollow Trail is said to turn spooky and sinister after the cloak of dusk falls.

disembodied footsteps in the dark. While many urban legends about Zombie Road are pure bunk, death has visited the trail and its environs from time to time. According to a 2012 piece in the *Riverfront Times*, a 19th-century woman was killed by a train here, and the area's rugged topography was a magnet for Native American ambushes on early settlers.

Now a paved trail, Zombie Road can still be visited before sunset, where it attracts the usual assortment of power-walking fitness enthusiasts.

But evening adventures are prohibited by law and police do enforce the rules. Whether or not something supernatural prowls these environs at night, the authorities of this world certainly do—and many a thrillseeker has an expensive citation to prove it.

North County's Carrico Road was a similar target for ghost-hunting teens for years due to legends of alleged "bubbleheads" who lived there.

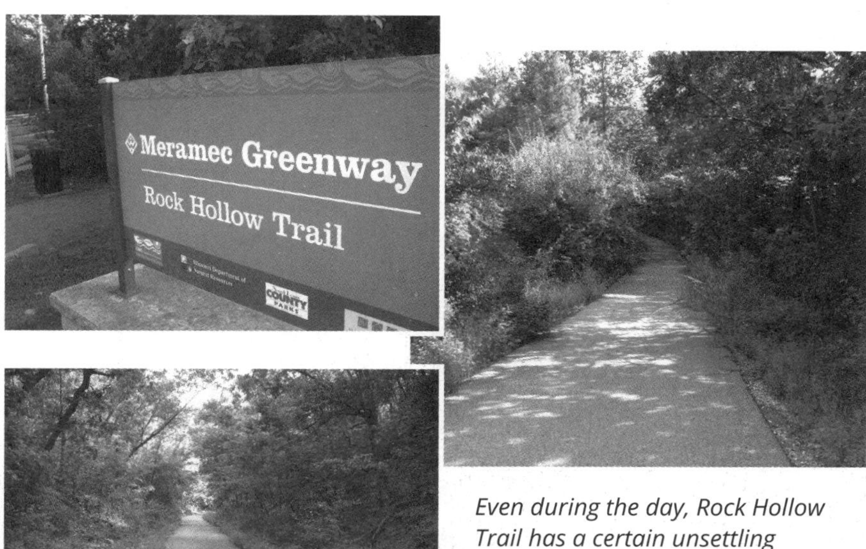

Even during the day, Rock Hollow Trail has a certain unsettling desolation to it, isolated far from traffic noise and distant from most human habitation.

25 WHERE THE CORAL COURT LIVES ON

Where can you still find an original façade from St. Louis's most infamous motel?

Regrettably, the Coral Court reached its checkout time in 1995, when preservationists couldn't stop a date with the wrecking ball. But the iconic glass-and-brick visage of St. Louis's "no-tell" motel hasn't vanished entirely from our fair city.

At the Museum of Transportation, the cream-hued façade from an original unit of the roadside inn of ill-repute has been lovingly reassembled for its adoring fans as part of the area's rich Route 66 motoring heritage.

Moreover, the Coral Court is far from the only bit of history to be found at this hidden gem in West County. Only a few feet away, there is a rare turbine-driven car that can run on anything from whiskey to corn oil. The vehicle

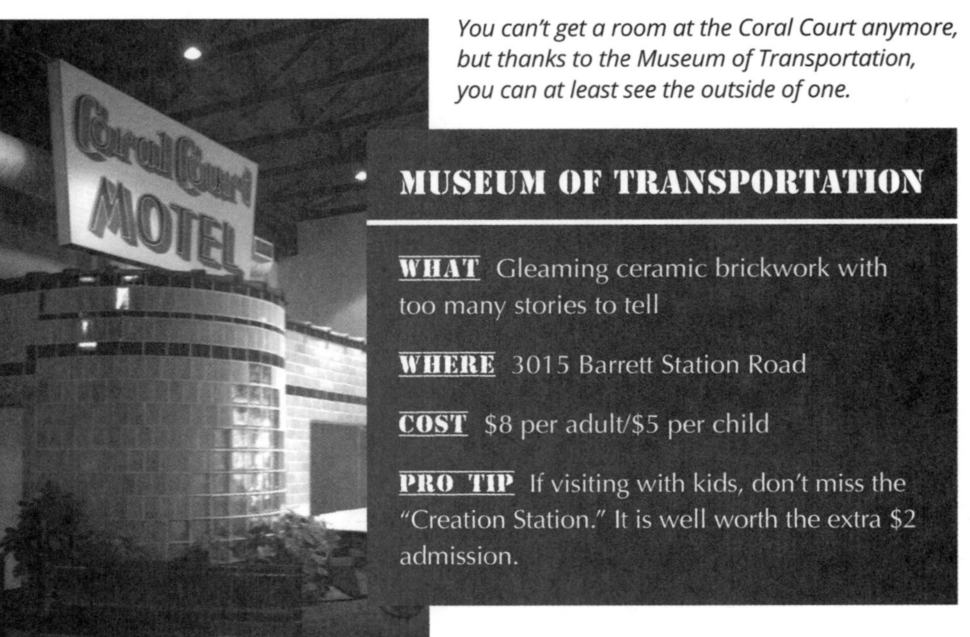

You can't get a room at the Coral Court anymore, but thanks to the Museum of Transportation, you can at least see the outside of one.

MUSEUM OF TRANSPORTATION

WHAT Gleaming ceramic brickwork with too many stories to tell

WHERE 3015 Barrett Station Road

COST $8 per adult/$5 per child

PRO TIP If visiting with kids, don't miss the "Creation Station." It is well worth the extra $2 admission.

was sought after by talk show giant Jay Leno, who even autographed the engine. Other oddities include the world's biggest tanker train carriage, a working streetcar, one of the area's earliest mobile phones, and a tricked-out "dream car" lacquered with diamond-infused paint and used by singing sensation Bobby Darin.

Driven by a single-cylinder engine, one 1901 specimen in the museum's collection was built by the St. Louis Motor Carriage Company.

Signed by Jay Leno, Chrysler's turbine-driven vehicle (top left) is a popular attraction at the museum, but the institution isn't just focused on vintage cars. An extensive collection of rail items complements displays on sea and air travel as well.

26 THE INVISIBLE TOWN

How did a bizarre failed stadium proposal give birth to St. Louis's smallest and weirdest municipality?

Even in a metro area famously defined by miniature towns, the tiny Village of Champ stands out as an oddity. With less than a square mile of territory, barely any roads, and just 13 residents, this North County city tucked against the I-70/270 interchange has no municipal services. Its main street also serves as the entrance to a church parking lot, and the city limit isn't even marked by signs. Champ doesn't have a city hall, a police department, or a website. Even many lifelong St. Louisans don't know it exists. A large portion of the town is taken up by a landfill and—as the *Riverfront Times* drily noted in 2001—the five people on the board of trustees represented half the city's adult population.

So where did this strange place come from—and why is it named "Champ"?

The answer is Bill Bangert, a frighteningly energetic and charmingly eccentric businessman who spent much of his life blurring the line between visionary civic boosterism and sheer lunacy. A fanatically athletic former Berkeley mayor who ran for numerous offices under at least three different party labels,

---

CHAMP

WHAT A very puny muni

WHERE Along Creve Coeur Mill Road near Grace Church

COST Free

PRO TIP No signs mark Champ's borders. Type the name into Google Maps to find their exact location.

Bangert once bet a Scottish mayor that he could carry two stones weighing nearly 800 pounds across a bridge. He won.

Jessica Adele Court has the dual distinction of being both the main road in Champ and of having more letters in its name than the town has residents.

he once proposed building an island at the confluence of the Missouri and Mississippi Rivers with a giant fountain on it and wanted not only to bring the Olympics to St. Louis but to compete in them. He billed himself as "the world's strongest mayor" in honor of his notable physique. As befits any larger-than-life political character, he once even survived an apparent assassination attempt.

But Champ was Bangert's oddest and most ambitious venture. The town's 1959 incorporation was part of an unusual financing blueprint to issue bonds and build a massive domed stadium with a huge restaurant hanging from its roof and attach it to the country's largest shopping complex. Bangert wound up in financial ruin due to the grandiose scheme, which ultimately fell apart. The town's moniker either came from its sports-related purpose or the surname of one of its investors.

Despite his failure, Bangert's ideas may not have been as off the wall as one thinks. Domed stadiums—of which Bangert's would have been the first in the nation—and suburban shopping malls did eventually take off. So did development in nearby Earth City and at Riverport, which, while not as ambitious as Bangert's plan, did put an entertainment venue near present-day Champ. Moreover, his bond scheme, novel at the time, was similar to tax-increment financing, which became popular later. His wild idea may have even frightened leaders in the City of St. Louis enough to encourage the 1966 construction of Busch Stadium in a bid to retain the baseball Cardinals downtown.

Whatever the case, the ever-enthusiastic Bangert, who died in 2011, said he never had any regrets and still considered Champ among his greatest accomplishments.

27 BIRTH OF A BEVERAGE

Is the invention of 7Up connected to St. Louis?

Local folks know that St. Louis has a proud soft-drink heritage, and most can define it in one word: Vess.

Indeed, this iconic local soda maker did get its start here. Now owned by beverage enterprise Cott, Vess's prominence in the area is immortalized by the large green lemon-lime bottle visible from Interstate 70 as you come into downtown.

But St. Louis played a part in the creation of a much bigger entry in the lemon-lime market. Soft drink inventor Charles Leiper Grigg got his start at Vess marketing Whistle, the orange-flavored thirst quencher still popular in the company's lineup. However, after parting ways with the company, he wanted to develop a competitor to Whistle. He did just that, labeling it with the friendly name "Howdy."

THE VESS BOTTLE

WHAT An oversized alternative to colas

WHERE 520 O'Fallon Street

COST None

NOTEWORTHY Vess, located in Maryland Heights, was bought out by its new owner in 1994 for more than $27 million.

Originally, 7Up contained lithium. No longer in the soda, it is still used as a pharmaceutical to stabilize moods.

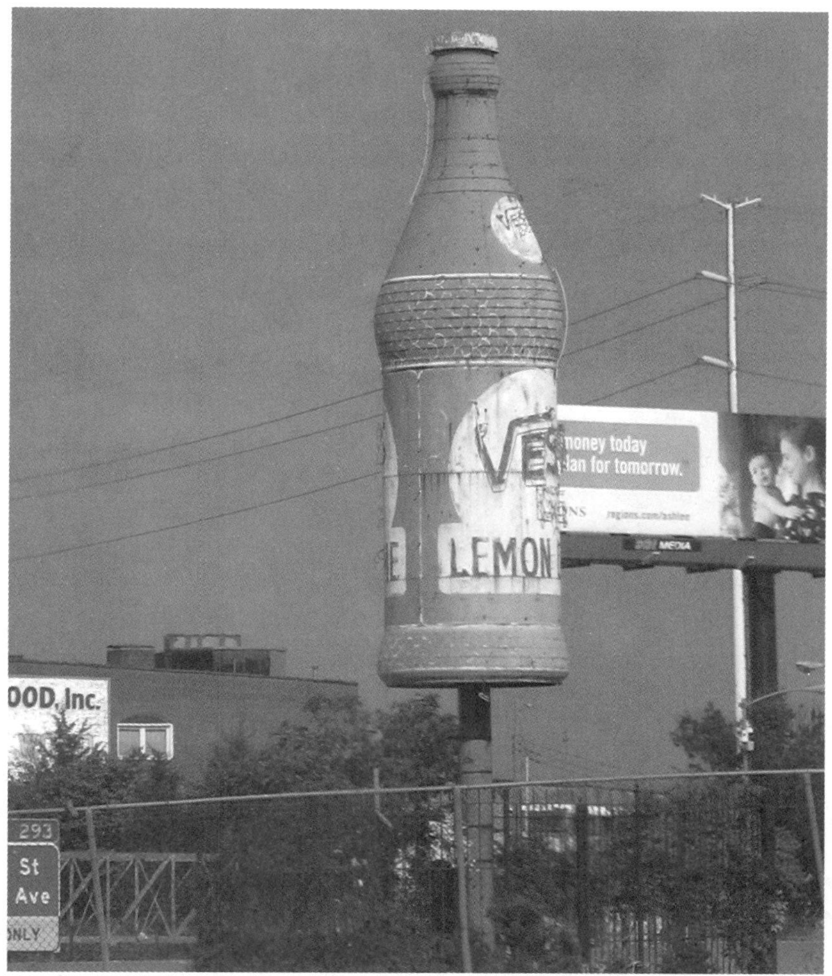

This huge bottle was originally erected in 1953, but it was initially planted on the Southside. It acquired its current downtown digs in the late 1980s.

Yet the Howdy Corporation also came up with a second contribution to the market. In 1929, Grigg stamped it with the rather hefty title "Bib-Label Lithiated Lemon-Lime Soda."

These days we just call it 7Up. Regrettably, the origins of that bubbly moniker remain enigmatic. Theories abound, ranging from the number of ingredients in the concoction to Grigg's good fortune in a poker game. The tale of its true genesis apparently died with its inventor.

28 FOR THE BIRDS . . .

Where is your best chance at seeing a bald eagle in the wild?

From the moment you walk into the visitors' center, there isn't much doubt about what the Audubon Center at Riverlands does. Model avians hang from the ceiling as though frozen while wheeling overhead. Quotes extolling birds emblazon the backs of benches. Charts and exhibits detail every habit of our fine feathered friends. Even the floor of the facility is a giant map of migratory bird routes.

Riverlands is aptly named, resting in the narrow neck of St. Charles County where the Missouri and Mississippi rivers meet in marshes that can only be described as a kind of natural Motel 6 for birds navigating the Mississippi Flyway, a well-traveled avian interstate in the sky bound for

All things avian can be found just north of the St. Louis suburbs thanks to the Riverlands Migratory Bird Sanctuary.

AUDUBON CENTER AT RIVERLANDS

WHAT A place to un"birden" the soul

WHERE 301 Riverlands Way, West Alton, Mo.

COST Free as a bird

PRO TIP As much as people might love the eagles, serious birders also adore the majestic trumpeter swans, which are considered to be among the area's most sought-after feathered guests.

points north. Egrets and herons are common guests in the wetlands surrounding the center, which overlooks 3,700 acres of migratory bird sanctuary run by the Army Corps of Engineers. A nearby 8.5-mile walking trail gives visitors front-row seats to the visiting birds that make Missouri their temporary home as the weather warms or cools.

And yes, you might indeed catch a glimpse of our national symbol taking wing. Bald eagles have been known to make an appearance in the wetlands.

At least 300 different species of bird might call Riverlands their home at one point or another.

Whether you are a serious avian enthusiast or just someone who likes pretty birds, the Audubon Center is just the place to get your feathered fix.

29 CIRCLE OF THE SEASONS

Where can you view St. Louis's oldest calendar?

One of the great untold tragedies of our unique city is the destruction of its native heritage and the erasure of so much of what the Mississippian cultures left behind. Thankfully, not all of those treasures have been forgotten. That's especially true on the Illinois side of the river, where urban development was less extensive and the massive earthworks at Cahokia Mounds were preserved for future generations.

But among the array of mounds is an oft-ignored work of scientific mastery all its own. Woodhenge lies just blocks from the main complex yet lacks none of its grandeur.

As of 2015, Cahokia, along with the Statue of Liberty, is one of only 10 cultural locations in the U.S. included on UNESCO's list of World Heritage Sites.

WOODHENGE

WHAT An ancient ceremonial site and calendar

WHERE The north side of Collinsville Road between Route 111 and the entrance to Cahokia Mounds

COST Free

NOTEWORTHY Red cedar, thought sacred by the inhabitants, was used for the posts at Woodhenge.

Interpretative programs are still done at the Woodhenge site near the equinoxes and solstices that were so central to the calendar's purpose.

Though it is a re-creation of the original structure, the posts representing this pre-Columbian solar calendar have been placed precisely as they would have been some 800 to 900 years ago.

In fact, Woodhenge is one of five such time-marking devices which once existed in the ancient city of Cahokia. This one is aligned with the huge Monks Mound such that sunrise on the equinox makes the sun look as though it is rising out of the great mound.

30 THE LEGENDARY LION

Where was the original Lion's Choice?

There are some things St. Louisans just naturally take for granted: Friendly Midwesterners. Cardinal playoff appearances. Provel cheese. That's why we so often forget that every city in America isn't necessarily blessed with the sorts of wonders that we enjoy every day.

Think of that the next time you bite into the signature seasoned meat at your nearby Lion's Choice, an establishment that has watered the mouths of Gateway City carnivores for as long as anyone can remember. It is indeed a local chain, and you can still dine at the very first restaurant at which St. Louis residents got a taste of the succulent red-tinged "roasted beef," which has since become famous.

The red hue was actually a part of one of the restaurant's early names. Founded in 1967, it was first known as Brittany Beef but soon switched to Red Lion Beef House. That later evolved into the present Lion's Choice. Even after the name shed its red color, the famous lion of that shade remains indelibly linked to one of St. Louis's most well-established local eateries.

The typical Lion's Choice location cranks out 60,000 pounds of its famous beef annually.

THE FIRST LION'S CHOICE

WHAT The original spot for a St. Louis original

WHERE 14919 Manchester Road

COST Depends on how hungry you are

PRO TIP Lion's Choice may be best known for its sandwiches, but some of its dessert options are worth exploring as well. The restaurant is famous for its tiny—and highly affordable—mini-cones, either plain or dipped in an irresistible chocolate shell.

Traditionally, Lion's Choice preferred the term "roasted beef" rather than "roast beef," as it wished to stress the process of roasting its product over time. Either way you want to say it though, you can still enjoy the result at Lion's Choice's original Ballwin location.

31 FLORISSANT'S HIDDEN CEMETERY

Just what is a Spanish land grant and why is a park named after it?

The patch of ground at the corner of St. Ferdinand and St. Denis in Florissant is a nice enough stretch of land—grassy and pleasant, albeit empty in a nondescript sort of way.

But the name might prompt questions, and the ground holds a bit of a secret. The remains of some of the city's earliest settlers and founders rest beneath it.

In fact, this small park has a big history, having played a prominent role for early residents, who received the plot as a grant from the Spanish king. As a small village grew on the site, so did a church at St. Ferdinand and St. Louis streets. The associated graveyard saw the burial of many of those who first lived and worked on the land.

The church was eventually replaced in 1821 by a beautiful structure nearby that can still be seen today. The headstones were eventually removed—but not all of the

SPANISH LAND GRANT PARK

WHAT A pretty park, a historical treasure, and an unmarked graveyard

WHERE The corner of St. Ferdinand and St. Denis streets

COST Free

PRO TIP Be sure to visit the nearby Old St. Ferdinand Shrine on St. Charles Street. (See facing page for more information.)

This unusually named park has a great deal of history behind it, most of which is unknown to those who enjoy it today.

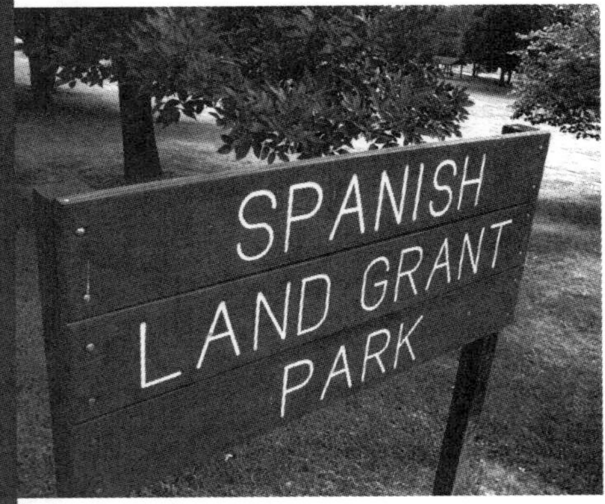

graves were—a fact confirmed by 21st-century excavations of the site that also unearthed a trove of thousands of artifacts ranging from coins to coffins.

Spanish Land Grant Park isn't just a nice place for a picnic or barbecue. It also holds an irreplaceable piece of the past, and some of the town's first citizens still reside forever under its sod.

The Spanish also used the area of today's park as a military drilling ground at one point.

Spanish Land Grant Park isn't the only item of historical interest in Old Town Florissant. Just a block over off St. Charles Street is the Old St. Ferdinand Shrine. With its cornerstone laid in 1821, the church predates downtown's famous Old Cathedral and holds the title of the second-oldest church building still standing in the St. Louis area. Between the two landmarks is the Florissant Community Garden and Pollinator Park (at right), sponsored through a partnership with the St. Louis Zoo.

32 THE ULTIMATE SACRIFICE

Why is there a huge ship anchor on Chestnut Street?

St. Louisans are accustomed to unusual sights in the city. Yet few things could stand out quite as vividly as the nine-ton boat anchor at the corner of Chestnut and 13th streets. Still, not many take much time to notice the nautical relic.

They should make the effort. The anchor, formerly of the WWII-era *USS Langley* aircraft carrier, was dedicated on Independence Day in 1999 to mark the Soldiers' Memorial, a facility oft-mentioned but all-too-frequently undervisited by St. Louisans. That's too bad because what's inside is worth a look.

Originally conceived in the 1920s as a tribute to those who had lost their lives in the First World War, it was more than a decade before President Franklin Roosevelt came to dedicate the site for construction, and it didn't open its doors until 1938, just as humanity stood on the brink of another

THE ANCHOR

WHAT A nine-ton reminder of those who gave their all

WHERE 1315 Chestnut Street

COST Free

PRO TIP Soldiers Memorial has rooms and other spaces available for rent to groups for various events, particularly for veterans' organizations and schools. Inquire regarding rates.

This massive piece of naval history that now enjoys its retirement on a downtown street corner served aboard a carrier that received nine battle stars during its active service in the Pacific and European theaters.

Above, the "Silent Table" features various symbols commemorating POWs and MIAs,including a lemon, which recognizes a prisoner's bitter fate, salt for a family's tears, and an inverted glass to show a toast that cannot be shared. Exhibits at the museum are wide-ranging, covering all branches of service and rotating regularly.

planetwide conflict. Late Mayor Bernard Dickmann called it a "place of love and a monument of peace."

Inside are exhibits that educate on both the tools and the cost of war—many with a focus on local veterans or ships of interest to the area. In addition to a torpedo and other items, there is a model of the *USS Missouri* attack submarine as well as specifications for the cruiser *USS St. Louis*. The "Lucky Lou" was noted for the quick reaction of its crew during the attack on Pearl Harbor, where it narrowly avoided both torpedo attack and aerial assault, becoming the only ship to escape the harbor during the bombing. The vessel, which suffered no casualties in the attack, went on to earn 11 battle stars in the Pacific. Despite a number of close scrapes—the Japanese reported sinking the stubborn ship three times—the *St. Louis* survived the war.

The limestone figures with horses representing Courage, Vision, Loyalty, and Sacrifice were sculpted by St. Louisan Walker Hancock.

33 THE GIANT EYEBALL

What is the significance of the huge eye at Laumeier Sculpture Park?

Sometimes you just have the feeling that someone is watching.

Thanks to artist Tony Tasset, that's not always an easy sensation for West Countians to shake.

With a circumference of more than 37 feet, Tasset's *Eye*, a fiberglass, steel, and resin creation modeled on the artist's own anatomy, has been greeting—and sometimes vaguely creeping out—visitors at Laumeier Sculpture Park since 2007.

So what does it mean?

Complete with spidery red blood vessels, the Cincinnati native's work is meant to convey commonality by using something "unique, individual and emblematic," according to the park's online description of the piece, which notes

Many love to browse the art at Laumeier, but not just any piece of art can browse back.

LAUMEIER SCULPTURE PARK

WHAT Art that observes you back

WHERE 12580 Rott Road

COST Free

PRO TIP While wandering the park's grounds, don't forget to check into the institution's educational programming opportunities at the newly revamped Kranzberg Education Lab. Special programs are available for schools and educators.

that it works to address "how we engage and perceive each other while concurrently asserting a prophetic, perhaps even omniscient, presence."

Incidentally, St. Louis isn't the only city to feel that presence. Other Tasset eyes have popped up in Chicago and Dallas, the latter having a three-story version.

A huge eye may not appeal to everyone, but in a 2010 interview regarding his ocular art, that seemed okay with Tasset. The artist said that his worst fear would be if his piece generated no emotion at all. "I've always wanted to make work that people either loved or hated," he said.

Though many enunciate it as "law," the "lau" in the park's name actually rhymes with "now" or "cow."

Unusual, quirky, or thought-provoking, the selection of pieces on display at Laumeier is never dull. A trip through the park has something for everyone. Some exhibits even have touchable representations of work being presented for the visually impaired. For those seeking a more physically active experience, take one of the special art hikes on trails that twist through the park.

34 MARY OF THE MISSISSIPPI

Did a miracle once save a tiny St. Charles County town from disaster?

At first glance, it might seem unusual. After all, there is no special connection between the Virgin Mary and anything related to waterways.

That is, unless you live in Portage Des Sioux.

For that small St. Charles County town hugging the Mississippi, the religious icon is forever known as "Our Lady of the Rivers," a name emblazoned on a statue of her that gazes watchfully over pleasure craft and barges alike to this day.

The story of Mary's special connection to the area goes back to the deadly flood season of 1951, when the

OUR LADY OF THE RIVERS

WHAT A religious icon

WHERE Portage Des Sioux

COST Free

PRO TIP Push the button on the door of the shrine to hear more about the area's history.

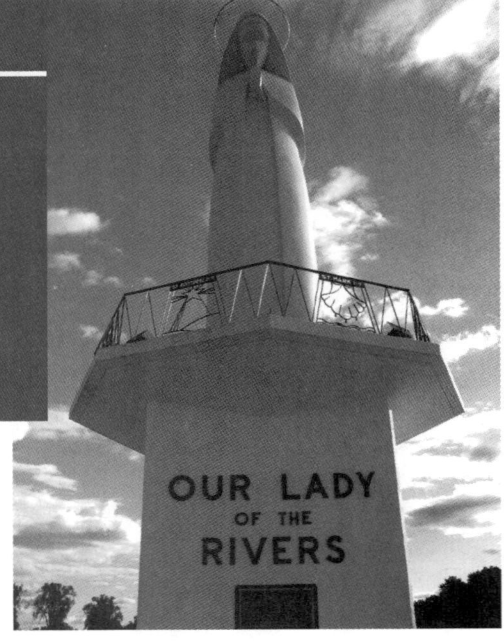

Erected in 1957, this 25-foot-tall representation of the Virgin Mary has long been adored by the residents of Portage Des Sioux, who believe she parted the raging waters on their behalf.

Missouri River to the south threatened to top its banks. Residents responded with prayer. Eventually, the weakened levees did fail, leaving the overflow to wash across the exposed bottomland toward the Mississippi. Yet, seemingly through divine intervention, the waters split, flowing to either side of the town and preserving it. In gratitude, residents erected this shrine to the Blessed Virgin, whose haloed visage stares out at the waters to this day.

According to legend, the town was named for a group of Sioux that moved their boats through the area to escape a rival band of Indians.

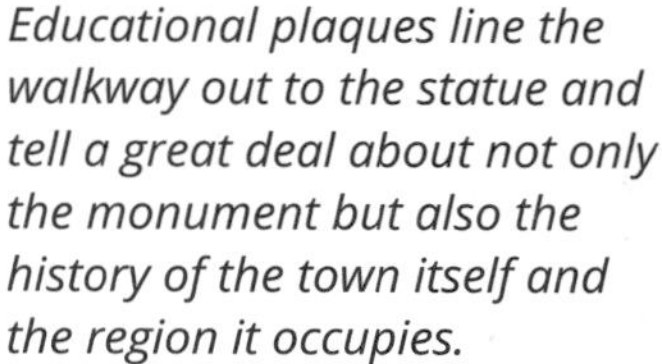
Educational plaques line the walkway out to the statue and tell a great deal about not only the monument but also the history of the town itself and the region it occupies.

35 ORIGINS OF THE FREEWAY

Did the interstate system really begin in St. Charles?

When you think about it, the title is quite impressive. The planet's greatest highway system was indeed born right here in the area. A busy stretch of I-70 in St. Charles just across the Blanchette Bridge is commemorated as the first interstate project to start construction.

But of course, like any good claim to fame, there is a fair measure of dispute.

In fact, a sign outside of Topeka, Kan., claims its part of I-70 as the first project completed under the auspices of the Federal-Aid Highway Act. It isn't a completely invalid boast either. The construction initiative had actually already

---

Named for St. Charles's founder Louis Blanchette, the I-70 bridge was dedicated in 1958.

SITE OF THE FIRST INTERSTATE

WHAT The genesis of everyone's morning commute

WHERE Westbound I-70 just before the Route 94 exit

COST Free. (Well, your tax dollars already paid for it anyway).

PRO TIP There is no stopping on the interstate, so this is one historic site you'll need to enjoy at 60 m.p.h.

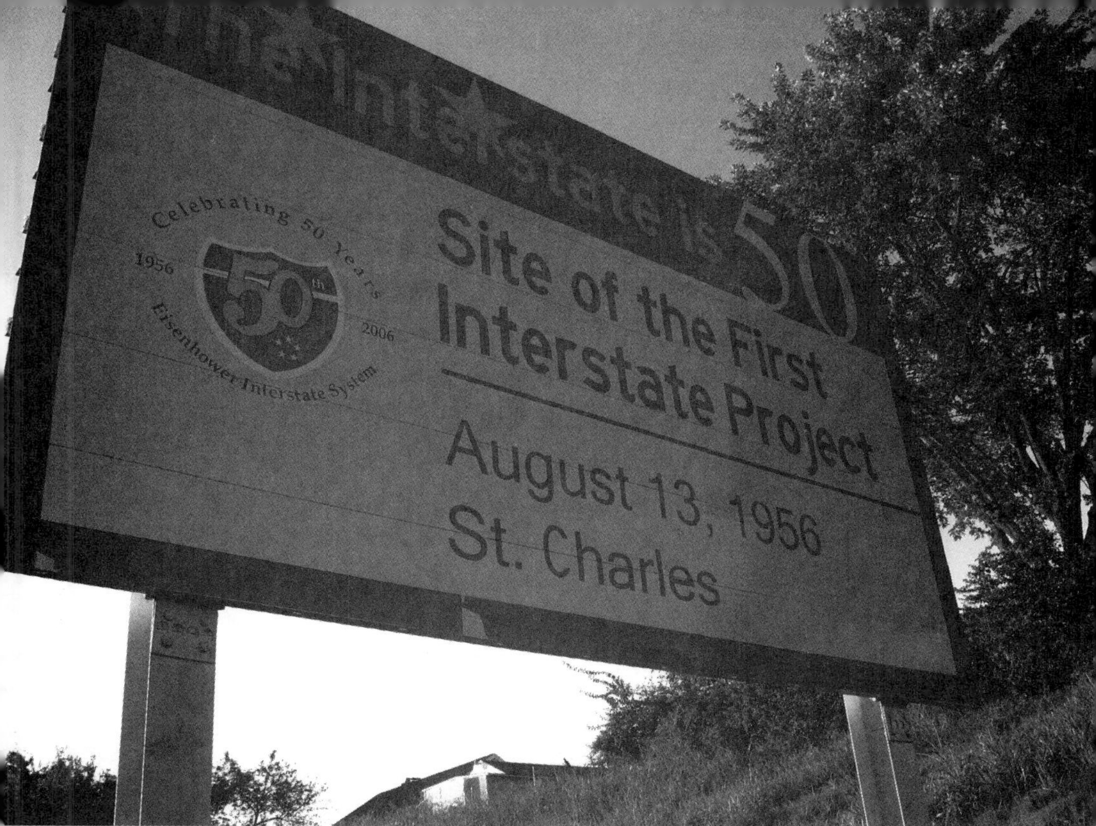

This sign is correct, but "firsts" are a tricky business. Both Kansas and Pennsylvania also have claims on being the true birthplace of the interstate system.

begun there before the act was signed, although the federally funded paving didn't get going until September.

But there's actually a third claimant to the title, and this one predates not just the other two but the highway act itself—by over a decade and a half. That's the Pennsylvania Turnpike, which began accepting traffic in 1940. Though the name "interstate" wasn't in use yet, the new road was basically the first in the nation to premiere the concept of a long-distance, limited-access highway. In effect, it was an interstate before interstates existed.

36 IF THE SHOE FITS . . .

Why is there a giant shoe made of other shoes in Clayton?

"It's hard to be emotional about a brown shoe," noted the company's CEO in a *Post-Dispatch* article during a rebranding of the enterprise as Caleres in 2015. But for generations of St. Louisans, Brown Shoe has held an emotional connection to the city since its creation in the late 19th century.

Its famous "shoe of shoes" wasn't a fixture in Clayton for quite that long. The quirky 1.5-ton artwork of aluminum footwear took up its duties in front of the corporate headquarters in 2000. The brainchild of Victoria Fuller, it was on display at City Museum before the move to

---

THE SHOE OF SHOES

WHAT A giant shoe made of non-giant shoes

WHERE 8300 Maryland Avenue

COST Free to view but not available in your size

NOTEWORTHY Caleres also owns Dr. Scholl's and Famous Footwear.

The Brown in Brown Shoe comes from George Warren Brown, the same name on Washington University's Social Work School.

the county. Its most recent relocation came as part of the corporate rebranding that is set to transform the front entrance of the old Brown building into a more modernistic creation. Fuller's giant footwear, composed of 2,000 shoes, has been moved to the side of the structure.

As for Caleres—a label derived from a variant of the Latin for "to glow"—it moves onward. The brand has been increasingly expanding into other segments of fashion and, according to media reports, had a reported value of $2.6 billion as of 2015.

No word on the size, but one imagines this Clayton creation would be even less comfortable to wear than regular high heels.

37 KINDERGARTEN'S KICKOFF

How did St. Louis premiere an educational advancement that every modern American family takes for granted?

St. Louis didn't invent kindergarten in the United States. But the fact that you and your children were able to attend one is probably attributable to a St. Louisan.

The first American kindergarten was established in Wisconsin before the Civil War by a Hamburg-born woman who introduced the German concept to Americans for the first time. But that effort was privately funded. Adding kindergarten as a concept to the public school system took the efforts of educational pioneer Susan Blow, who created the first public kindergarten in the United States on St. Louis's Southside in 1873.

Today, you can still visit Blow's educational innovation at the old Des Peres School Building, which now houses the

DES PERES SCHOOL

WHAT The start of public kindergarten

WHERE 6303 Michigan Avenue

COST Free

PRO TIP Check out the nearly 1,200 photos of area servicemen and women that line the walls of this building, which is now home to the Carondelet Historical Society.

This building on Michigan Avenue is why you had to start school a year earlier than you probably wanted to.

Carondelet Historical Society. The society has kept Blow's model classroom in pristine condition and has a wide assortment of items on display that early teachers would have used to convey ideas like colors and shapes to their pupils.

A decade after Blow's pilot project, kindergarten had spread throughout St. Louis's public school system. The rest of the country wouldn't be far behind.

The city's first school board was formed in 1833, just 12 years after Missouri attained statehood.

Few things escape the watchful eye of the teacher in this classroom. A visitor can also view a wide range of early educational aids, known as "gifts." But there is much more to the Carondelet Historical Society than its history with public kindergarten. At right, you can see the ever-expanding wall of honor recognizing military veterans. There's also a full research library on-site and friendly staff to help patrons.

38 THE GREAT BIRD OF ALTON

Why does a fearsome creature haunt this riverside rockface?

It stares out over the waters of the Mississippi with a vaguely unnerving grimace. Certainly, it doesn't look friendly. Nonetheless, the Piasa Bird remains a popular attraction along the Great River Road.

The first European to run into the dragonlike avian's imposing image was Jacques Marquette, who explored the area more than 300 years ago. Its origins were definitely Native American, although its later mythology about swooping down to gobble up men until a brave and crafty chieftain devised a plot to bring it down probably owed more to the early 19th-century embellishments of a Caucasian writer by the name of John Russell than to actual tribal legends.

THE PIASA BIRD

WHAT An ancient legend

WHERE Illinois Route 100 about a mile north of Alton

COST Free

PRO TIP The Piasa makes a wonderful stop on your journey, but don't forget to travel the River Road farther up, where the stunning bluffs make for a picture-perfect day trip.

Part dragon, part bird but all frightening, the Piasa has been a part of Illinois tradition since before the state existed.

The initial native artwork is long gone, but various iterations of the painted cryptid have graced the bluff over the years as the legends gained popularity. The identity of its originators remains unknown since the image predated European exploration of the area. Some sources suspect it may be a part of or related to the Cahokian culture that became so famous for its mound-building proclivities and gave St. Louis its traditional nickname of Mound City.

The Piasa rock face contains not only the mythical bird but also a number of caves due to extensive quarrying operations.

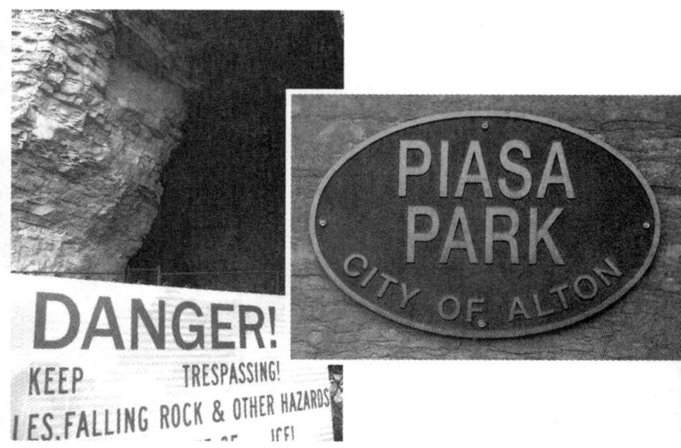

The Piasa story has long had a place in the cultural annals of the Alton area, whatever the source of the legend. But a number of Piasa Birds have stared icily from these cliff walls. The first attempts to restore the old artwork began in the 1920s with local men Herbert and Orland Forcade. A 1980s incarnation of the monster was done on a metal plate but that was later dropped in favor of painting the bluffs themselves once again. The metal version became a mascot for a high school in nearby Piasa, Illinois.

39 MAKING TRACKS ON HODIAMONT

What is this strange North St. Louis road with the odd name?

Parts of it are open to traffic. Other parts are blocked off completely. Some intersections are mysteriously marked "Hodiamont Tracks." Others aren't labeled at all. This unusual, alley-like road running between parks and backyards on the city's Northside has no addresses, but it does have a history—one bound up with a way of life that was once vital to St. Louis and which today is no more.

The last streetcar run for the Hodiamont line was car No. 1628, which ended its tenure—and the age of St. Louis trolleys—on May 21, 1966.

THE HODIAMONT RIGHT OF WAY

WHAT The right side of some very old tracks

WHERE Crossing north-south arteries from Hodiamont to just before Vandeventer

COST Alas, there's no fare anymore

PRO TIP Some parts are closed off. Others are private. Respect signs and barriers.

It is a strange enough name for a road, but this sign doesn't just mark a single street but the grave of an entire mode of transportation.

This is the Hodiamont Right-of-Way. Its unique name comes from its history. It's the old dedicated route for the Hodiamont line, one of countless streetcar routes that used to criss-cross the area. Evidence of most are gone now, but Hodiamont actually had a separate route for a significant part of its length, one which still survives as a chopped-up remnant running from Gwen B. Giles Park near Skinker north of Cabanne Avenue before twisting south at Union Boulevard and running just north of Enright before letting out onto that street a little shy of Vandeventer.The forgotten little road is a reminder of a network of rails that used to run from Belleville to Creve Coeur and today exists not at all.

40 DANIEL BOONE SLEPT HERE

What does this marker have to do with one of America's frontier heroes?

In the modern world, we often forget that today's humdrum suburb happens to have been yesterday's rugged wilderness. Such is the case with this otherwise nondescript, homey setting next to Wyman Elementary School at the corner of Wabaday and Kenosho avenues.

Most St. Louisans are probably familiar with Boone's more famous abode in St. Charles County, but he also stayed in present-day St. Louis County for a time when the Spanish still owned the area. The site of Boone's cabin is one of a surprising number of historical points of interest in the city of Overland, which was quite the stomping ground for pioneers in its heyday. Historical markers litter the municipality's side streets, as it was a convenient stopping point for the then-arduous journey from St. Louis to St. Charles.

BOONE'S CABIN

WHAT A cabin in the suburbs

WHERE The corner of Wabaday and Kenosho avenues

COST Free

PRO TIP Avoid visiting at the end of school hours unless you enjoy traffic.

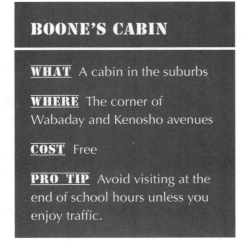

Boone's cabin was demolished in 1880.

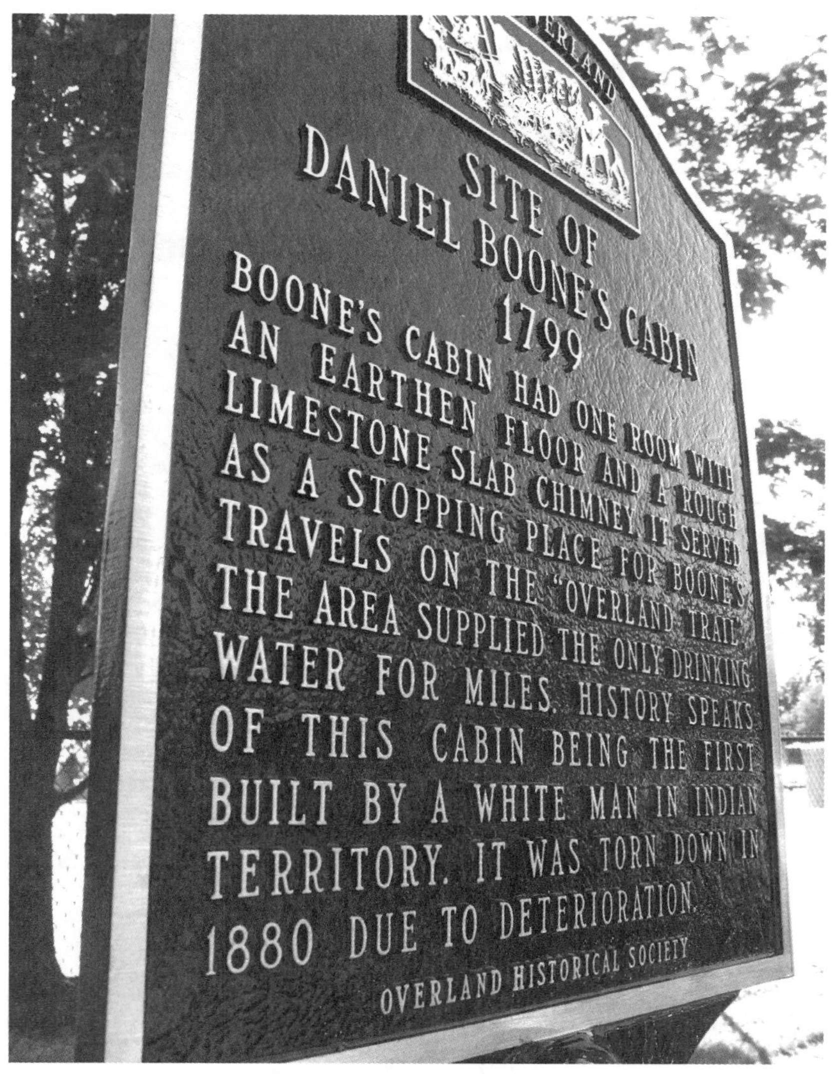

OVERLAND
SITE OF
DANIEL BOONE'S CABIN
1799
BOONE'S CABIN HAD ONE ROOM WITH
AN EARTHEN FLOOR AND A ROUGH
LIMESTONE SLAB CHIMNEY. IT SERVED
AS A STOPPING PLACE FOR BOONE'S
TRAVELS ON THE "OVERLAND TRAIL"
THE AREA SUPPLIED THE ONLY DRINKING
WATER FOR MILES. HISTORY SPEAKS
OF THIS CABIN BEING THE FIRST
BUILT BY A WHITE MAN IN INDIAN
TERRITORY. IT WAS TORN DOWN IN
1880 DUE TO DETERIORATION.
OVERLAND HISTORICAL SOCIETY

Today, children play at recess just a few yards from this notable piece of Overland history.

By the 1840s, a one-room school had been created that eventually became the basis for the Ritenour School District, which formed just after the Civil War.

Early pioneers would move through Overland on their way to the Santa Fe or Oregon trails. Early memorabilia and research from that era is still available at a reconstructed log house at 9711 Lackland Road.

41 FAME IN 64 SQUARES

Where can you see the world's biggest chess piece?

The Gateway City may only be a quarter of a millennia old, but this ancient game of strategy is taken quite seriously here, and nothing says "checkmate" quite like a chess piece as tall as a giraffe. Weighing in at over one ton, this big fellow isn't quite game-ready.

But what the world's largest chess piece may lack in subtlety, it makes up for in appropriateness. St. Louis is unquestionably the chess capital of the nation, and at the World Chess Hall of Fame, a wide range of exhibits, presentations, and displays featuring the greatest games and best players to ever grace the boards planetwide drive home the point quite nicely.

WORLD CHESS HALL OF FAME

WHAT A king who reigns supreme

WHERE 4652 Maryland Avenue

COST Free

PRO TIP Central West End parking is a chess game all its own. Good luck.

Made of plywood, this replica king is taller than two men, though they'd need to work together in order to move it anyway.

Here the game comes alive for those most passionate about it and, of course, as with any good hall of fame, there is a gift shop downstairs as well.

If this piece were put into actual use, it would take a board the size of two tennis courts to play the game.

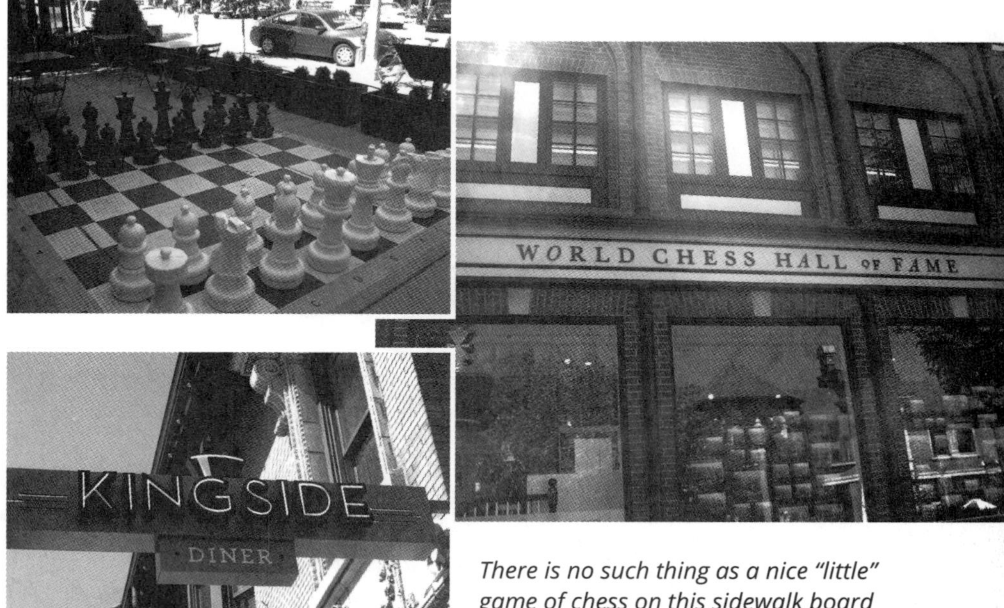

There is no such thing as a nice "little" game of chess on this sidewalk board outside the World Chess Hall of Fame. The institution began in 1986 but didn't move to St. Louis until 2011, when the city's growing notoriety for chess mastery began to attract attention. Meanwhile, even local businesses (above) have tried to capitalize on the area's burgeoning chess scene.

42 THE WORLD COMES TO ST. LOUIS

What is the Sinquefield Cup?

The name may be a mouthful, but the Chess Club and Scholastic Center of St. Louis really does need every syllable to tell you what they do. Right across the street from the sport's prestigious hall of fame, this is where the rubber meets the road. Large screens convey moves from games going on worldwide, while local players can sit considering strategies in their own contests. A casual play area is complemented by a tournament hall where competitors of all skill levels can compete in a more formal setting. A classroom and library are also on-site, with learning sessions taught by qualified staff or grandmasters and catering to everyone from children to those who wish to hone the art of real live tournament play.

CHESS CLUB AND SCHOLASTIC CENTER OF ST. LOUIS

WHAT All things chess-related

WHERE 4657 Maryland Avenue

COST $15 a month for adults (special rates also available)

PRO TIP Visitors are permitted one free visit to the facility.

Calling the Gateway City the chess capital of the country is no idle boast. The U.S. Senate passed a resolution confirming its status as such in 2014.

Then there is the Sinquefield Cup, the annual honor that attracts some of the planet's top names to go toe to toe. Named after philanthropist Rex Sinquefield, the race for the cup brought out eight of the ten highest-rated players in the chess universe in 2015.

The chess club has a membership of more than 1,200 and hosts more than 80 tournament events each year.

Founded in 2007, the club can convey games in real time from anywhere on Earth through cutting-edge technology. Meanwhile, casual play areas are available both indoors and out.

43 SHERMAN'S PRIDE

Why is there a tank kept in this Florissant park?

Florissant certainly seems a peaceable enough place, but if it ever decides to invade Hazelwood, it will have a decided advantage on its neighbor once it gets this classic vehicle back in working order.

So what's a Sherman tank doing in Bangert Park? For that, you can thank James "Jay" Russell Long, a Florissant resident and Marine veteran who contributed this beautiful specimen to the city in 1964. Sherman tanks were heavily used in WWII as well as the Korean War, but a few saw

THE BANGERT PARK TANK

WHAT An old soldier who hasn't faded away

WHERE 275 South New Florissant Road

COST Free

NOTEWORTHY Bangert Park, the oldest in Florissant, is home not just to a tank but to amenities ranging from horseshoe courts to a lighted roller hockey area.

In 2015, Lambert Airport lost its three pedestal display military jets to Whiteman Air Force Base after the move of the 131st Fighter Wing.

action even later. Some U.S. allies used the combat vehicles as late as the 1970s.

These days, the tank is a fixture at Bangert, where kids love to climb on its treads and turret. It seems a well-deserved retirement for this veteran of battles so long ago.

By a fitting coincidence, William Tecumseh Sherman, the Civil War general of whom this piece of impromptu playground equipment is the namesake, happens to be buried in St. Louis.

At one time, this war machine helped bring victory to the Allies over the scourge of fascism. Today, however, it has found new life bringing joy to children.

44 THIS OLD CHURCH

What is the oldest church in the region?

Some places truly stand the test of time. By any standard, Holy Family Church in Cahokia is one of those places. The simple log construction of its historic building has been standing on this spot since 1799, meaning it easily beats downtown's Old Cathedral by well over 30 years.

Though it predates the Louisiana Purchase, and although the house of worship was built nearly two decades before Illinois was established as a state, it was officially part of the United States during construction, since it lies east of the Mississippi River in what was then known as the Northwest Territory.

HOLY FAMILY CHURCH

WHAT The oldest church in the area

WHERE 116 Church Street, Cahokia, Illinois

COST It is free to view the building but donations are accepted

PRO TIP Regular tour hours are available during the summer months from Labor Day to Memorial Day. Tours are only by appointment.

The congregation was established three decades before St. Louis's founder Pierre Laclede was even born in France.

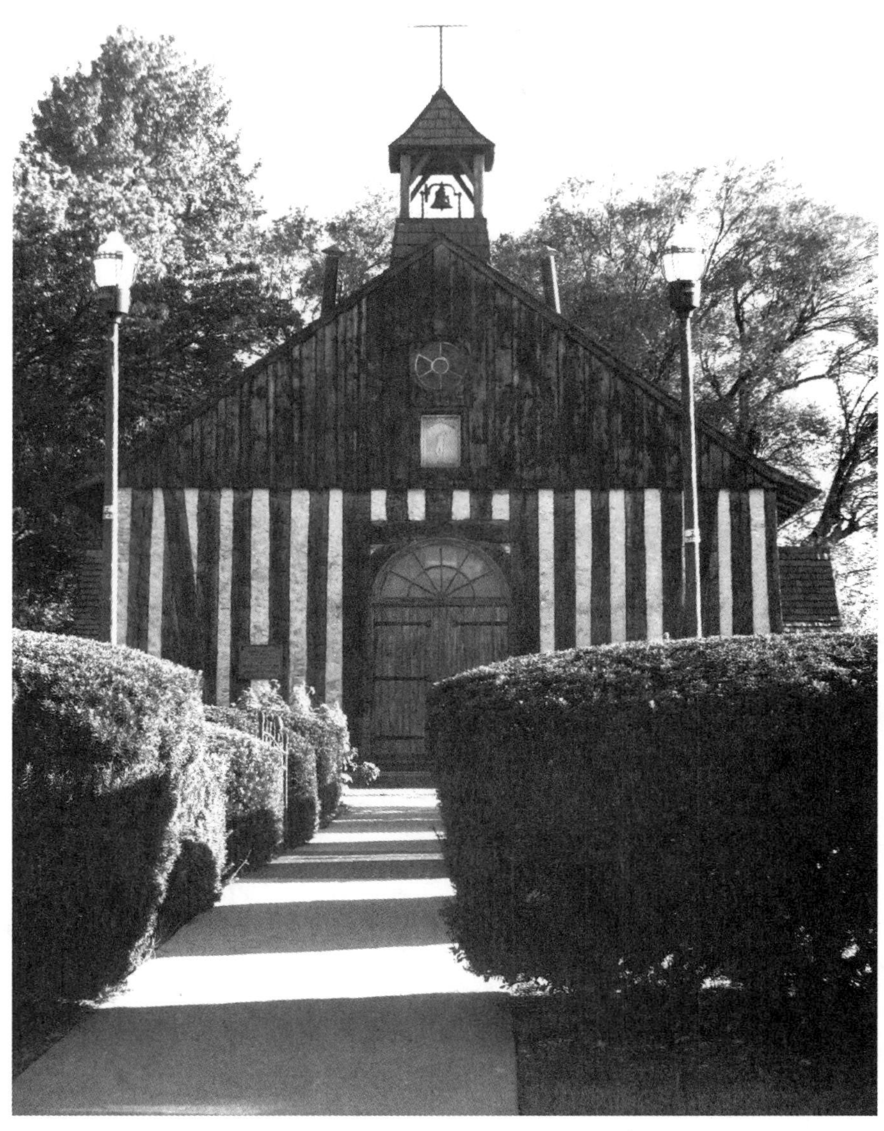

A Tridentine Latin Mass is still held in the confines of the old church each week at Holy Family.

The congregation, which now also uses a newer nearby facility for services, has quite a history as well. The Catholic parish itself has outdistanced its old church by a full century, having been founded in 1699, a time when the French were still exploring the region and George Washington's father was still a child.

45 ELIZA HOOLE IS NOT BURIED HERE

What's the story behind this gravestone in Tower Grove Park?

The etchings are so worn that they are barely discernible, but if you look closely enough, you can still make out the faint outline of the letters.

"Eliza Hoole," it reads. "1882."

This weather-beaten headstone wouldn't seem out of place in any historic cemetery. But this is no graveyard. It's a walking trail in Tower Grove Park where joggers and cyclists meander past. The marker's presence has long generated questions from puzzled park-goers, some of whom even stop to pay respects. The stone is strangely deserted, and Hoole's final resting place does not appear on an official map of the park.

ELIZA HOOLE'S MARKER

WHAT A non-gravestone

WHERE The southwest quadrant of the park near the Maury Pedestrian Gate

COST Free

PRO TIP If you can't find it, just ask any nearby jogger. They will probably know.

Second only to Forest Park in area, Tower Grove encompasses about 289 acres.

So just who was Eliza Hoole and how did she end up inexplicably buried in one of St. Louis's premier green spaces?

The short answer is that she didn't. This isn't a grave and Ms. Hoole isn't in it. The real story is that Hoole was a British cousin of Henry Shaw and this park was once his property. When Hoole planted a tree here, Shaw marked it with a monument that just happened to be shaped a bit like a headstone. The only giveaway is the word "oak" carved above Hoole's name. This is a marker for a living tree rather than a deceased person.

So, worry not. There is no need to tread lightly or leave flowers. This small stone commemorates a contribution Hoole made to the planet, not her departure from it.

Despite the impression this leaves, Eliza Hoole is not a permanent resident of Tower Grove Park.

46 THE RUINS OF ST. LOUIS

What are these strange ruins in Tower Grove Park?

The year 1867 was a regrettable one for the Lindell Hotel. The beautiful downtown structure burned in a massive late-March blaze. No one died but the building was a total loss.

Well, almost total. As it happened, St. Louis icon Henry Shaw was putting together a new park at the time and found himself in the market for some ancient ruins. After all, every good park needs ruins, and as it turns out, the lodging industry's loss was the park system's gain. The

When Shaw donated the land for Tower Grove, he stipulated that it "shall be used as a park forever."

THE LINDELL HOTEL

WHAT Ruins a bit newer than those found in Greece

WHERE Look for the fountain pond near the center of the park

COST Free

PRO TIP Examine the sooty build-up on the limestone as proof that these blocks were genuinely in a major fire.

Who doesn't love a nice set of ancient ruins, though—at only four years old—Shaw's version may have been a bit less ancient than most.

hotel may not have been the Acropolis, but its fire-singed limestone seemed the perfect complement to add a touch of rustic class to Tower Grove's nearby fountained lake.

So that's the story of how the short-lived Lindell Hotel found new life as a park adornment. And it's not the only bit of disused grandeur that Shaw borrowed from a local edifice. The Magnolia Entrance to the park is composed of columns scavenged from an 1870 remodel of a local county courthouse.

47 THE BIRTH OF THE BILLIKEN

Just what exactly is a Billiken and how did it become SLU's mascot?

Sports teams take great pride in their symbolism. In that, St. Louis University is no different. The Billiken mascot is just as beloved as the team. But where exactly did the idea of a Billiken come from?

The answer has complicated roots that seem to stretch back to a Kansas City artist, a Canadian poet, and a brief but intense turn-of-the-century fad for a unique good luck charm. The artist, Florence Pretz, first rendered the grinning character in a Canadian periodical in 1907 and patented it the following year. This set off something of a craze for Billiken items, statues, pins, songs, buttons, etc. For a short time, the Billiken was known worldwide. Its name evidently derived from a fanciful bit of colorful prose called "Mr. Moon, a Song of the Little People" by Bliss Carman, which was rife with such creative monikers as Thistledrift, Dewlap, and Meadowbee.

THE BILLIKEN STATUE

WHAT A happy good luck charm

WHERE Out front of Chaifetz Arena

COST Free

PRO TIP Purchasing a Billiken is said to bring luck but getting one as a gift is said to increase the effect.

In good seasons and bad, this charming Billiken's grin always warms the hearts of local SLU collegians.

Sadly, a business dispute, possibly over the meager royalties Pretz was receiving, seems to have soured the icon's creator a bit on her invention. She said she'd even smash one if she saw it.

But, though the Billiken's days as a planetary phenomenon have mostly past, the happy little fellow still finds a home in St. Louis, where his face continues to represent good luck as "the god of things as they ought to be." He even still has a presence around the world, even as far afield as Japan, where a representation of him graces a tower. There's also an annual Bud Billiken parade in Chicago.

Why the Billiken became linked specifically to SLU remains a matter of debate, but the most popular story is that the figure bore an uncanny resemblance to John Bender, the school's popular football coach.

Disbanded in 1949, SLU's long-defunct football team has one notable claim to fame. It threw the first forward pass in collegiate history.

The Billiken isn't the only example of statuary on the St. Louis University campus, which is noted for the many artistic figures that reside along its storied walkways and paths. The school is almost an outdoor art gallery all its own.

48 THE BIG APPLE

How did the Great Flood of 1993 inspire a 10-pound apple pie?

There are any number of commemorative markers and events to remember the courage and community-mindedness of people who pulled together to battle the raging waters of the Great Flood of 1993.

But few have immortalized the event quite like Mary Hostetter of The Blue Owl in Kimmswick, a tiny picturesque Jefferson County town less than 25 miles south of downtown St. Louis. It is there where patrons can experience the "Levee High Apple Pie," an astonishing 10-pound dessert containing roughly 18 apples. Hostetter's remarkable creation, which honors the levee that held back the waters during the deluge of that year, also comes in a caramel-pecan version just in case you don't quite get your fill from the regular. The dessert lover's delight has been featured everywhere from The Food Network to Oprah Winfrey's *O Magazine*.

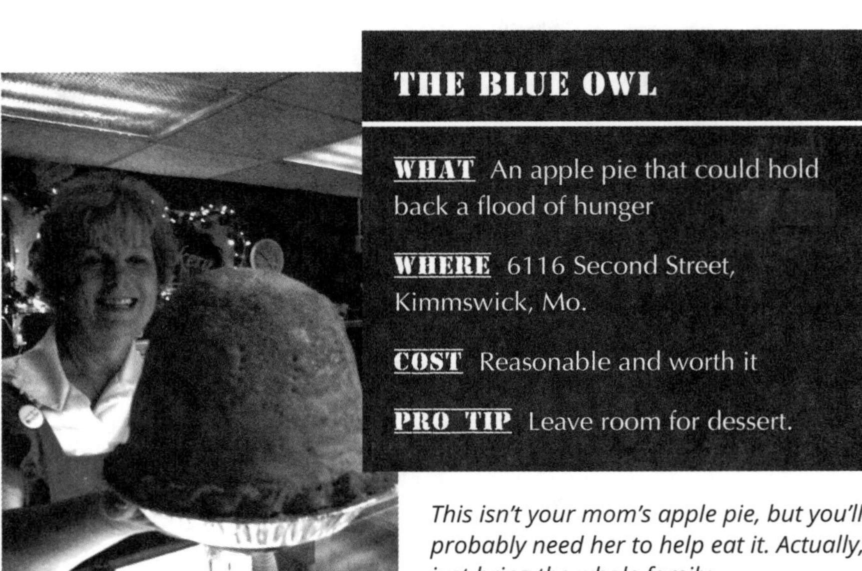

THE BLUE OWL

WHAT An apple pie that could hold back a flood of hunger

WHERE 6116 Second Street, Kimmswick, Mo.

COST Reasonable and worth it

PRO TIP Leave room for dessert.

This isn't your mom's apple pie, but you'll probably need her to help eat it. Actually, just bring the whole family.

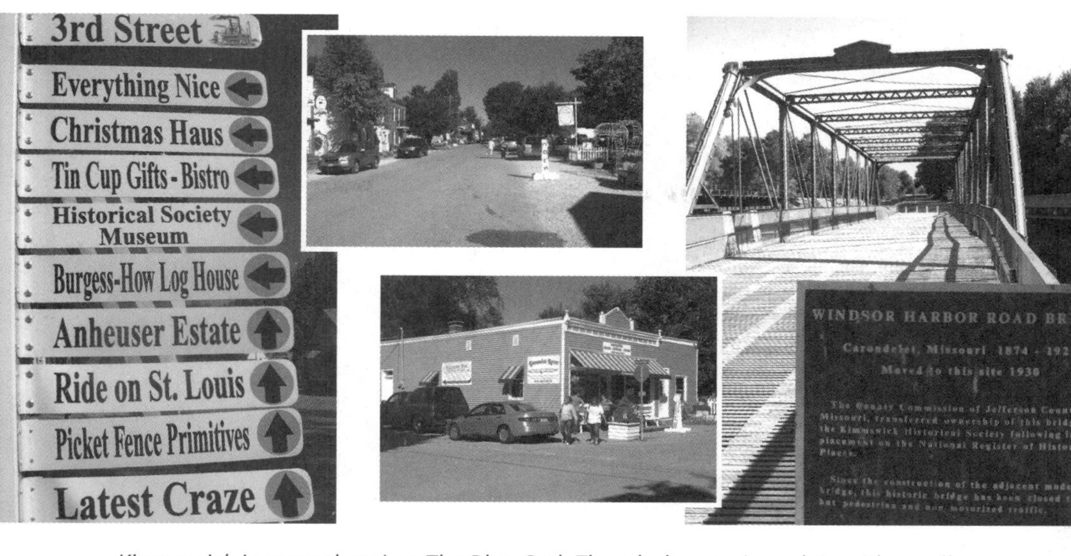

Kimmswick is more than just The Blue Owl. The whole area is replete with small shops. Don't forget a quick stop at the Windsor Harbor Road Bridge, a site on the National Register of Historic Places.

In fact, The Blue Owl itself has gained a fair share of notoriety for a homespun menu famous for far more than supersized apple pies.

Celebrating its 30th anniversary in 2015, the popular eatery grew initially out of a baked goods business Hostetter founded in the early 1980s, which became so successful that it saw her filling orders for 30,000 cookies for Christmas alone.

These days some 300 customers a day pour through the door, a figure that easily outstrips the population of the town itself. In 1997, the charming eatery earned its owner "Restaurateur of the Year" honors, and The Blue Owl has been noted various times in *Sauce Magazine's* Readers Choice Awards as well as earning mentions nationally on *The Today Show* and the Travel Channel.

Kimmswick was founded by Theodore Kimm, who probably added the ending "wick" in honor of his hometown of Brunswick, Germany.

49 KIMMSWICK'S BED OF BONES

Where can you meet a mastodon in Missouri?

Okay, so the big guy in the museum isn't an actual mastodon. He's a fiberglass representation based on various bones found outside the St. Louis area. However, these five-to-six-ton animals did indeed wander in prehistoric St. Louis and were even followed by the local population, the Clovis people, long before gooey butter cake and toasted ravioli were on the menu.

This fellow, standing about 10 feet tall, is one of the highlights of Mastodon State Historic Site, a lovely area in Jefferson County regarded by most residents for its pleasant camping and picnicking facilities. But the archeologically inclined can also learn a good deal about the region's prehistory on some of the local trails that pass by the Kimmswick Bone Bed, an area first examined in 1839 by Albert C. Koch, who, with a somewhat undue sense of

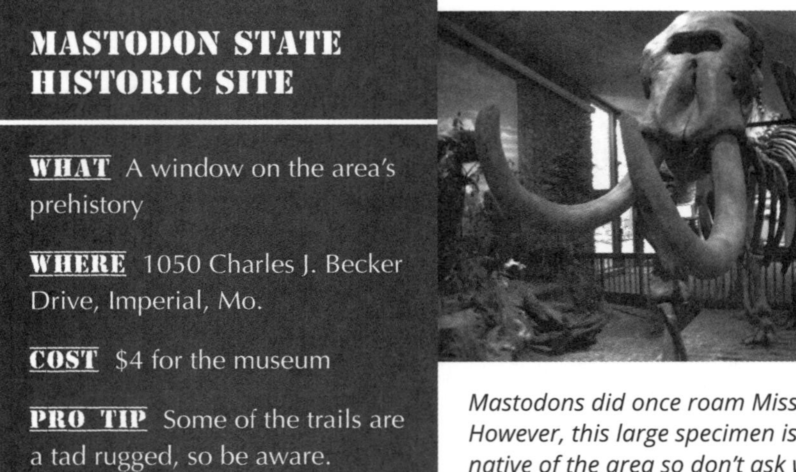

MASTODON STATE HISTORIC SITE

WHAT A window on the area's prehistory

WHERE 1050 Charles J. Becker Drive, Imperial, Mo.

COST $4 for the museum

PRO TIP Some of the trails are a tad rugged, so be aware.

Mastodons did once roam Missouri. However, this large specimen isn't a native of the area so don't ask what high school he went to. You'll just confuse him.

drama, termed the fossilized creatures he found there as "Missouri Leviathans."

Fortunately, by the 1970s, this historic site was saved for future generations through local efforts. The mastodons themselves weren't quite so lucky. They died out around 10,000 years ago.

Mastodons are not the same as mammoths, a similar animal that is more closely related to today's elephants.

Hiking trails are a prominent feature of Mastodon State Historic Site, which became associated with the state park system in 1976. Since then, nature enthusiasts have been able to enjoy both the fresh air and an education in the area's remarkably rich prehistory.

50 ST. LOUIS COUNTY'S FIRST ROAD

Why does this deserted two-lane street lead to a picnic table?

The pavement is there. Guardrails line the sides. Even the worn asphalt is still striped with a double yellow line. Yet, this road—clearly intended for cars—sits abandoned in a wooded area of North County rolling up a slope leading strangely to a picnic table on a bluff. What you are looking at is actually a piece of history. It is a section of an earlier version of the St. Charles Rock Road, a seemingly misnamed strip of pavement that has long mystified St. Louisans by neither leading to St. Charles nor being made of rock. In fact, it used to qualify on both counts. This deserted stretch a few yards from the current road's western terminus in Bridgeton runs to the former site of its long-gone bridge

Downtown's discontinuous St. Charles Street was once part of the St. Charles Rock Road.

RIVERWOODS PARK AND TRAIL

WHAT A piece of the county's first road

WHERE Make a left near the west end of the St. Charles Rock Road

COST Free

NOTEWORTHY In the olden days, the St. Charles Rock Road represented the eastern terminus of the famous Santa Fe Trail.

The St. Charles Rock Road is proof that paving surfaces come and go but names are forever.

over the Missouri River. At the peak of the slope is a lovely view of the 1.7-mile Riverwoods Trail, which runs through a nearby conservation and Missouri River wetlands area. The bluff where the bridge was turns out to be the perfect place for a picnic table—however incongruous one may seem. The associated 136 acres of green space runs all the way to Interstate 70.

As for the Rock Road itself, yes, it did used to be made of rock, acquiring its present name after being macadamized with stone at the close of the Civil War. Yet, the artery's history goes all the way back to when the Spanish created it as the first true road in what would become St. Louis County. It was probably established along a path already being blazed by wagons between the two bustling settlements, thus confirming, as frustrated North County drivers have long suspected, that traffic problems on the Rock Road existed before the road itself. In 1921, it also became the county's first concrete highway.

Amazingly, the Rock Road not only came before the United States' acquisition of the area but it is actually older than the nation itself, having been established in 1772.

51 LIBERTY THROUGHOUT THE LAND

What is that unusually shaped marker in Forest Park?

History, as they say, has a long memory. But sometimes, everyone needs a reminder of the past, and Forest Park is full of them. One of the most unique sits in the northeast corner of the park, right in view of the famous Chase Park Plaza. Centered on an American flag and perched on a raised platform of steps, the memorial seems to roll out like a scroll emblazoned with a mélange of quotes and evocative imagery.

But the story it tells is older than the city that surrounds it. What you are viewing is the Jewish Tercentenary Monument, a limestone commemoration of three centuries of Jewish life in what would ultimately become the United States of America, the nation with the largest Jewish population in the world. Erected in 1956, the stonework contains both Biblical verses and inscriptions honoring the freedoms that allowed Jews to flourish in the nation after their first arrival in 1654 in what was then the Dutch settlement of New Amsterdam.

The first Jews to arrive in America did so by accident. They were dropped off in New York after being rescued at sea.

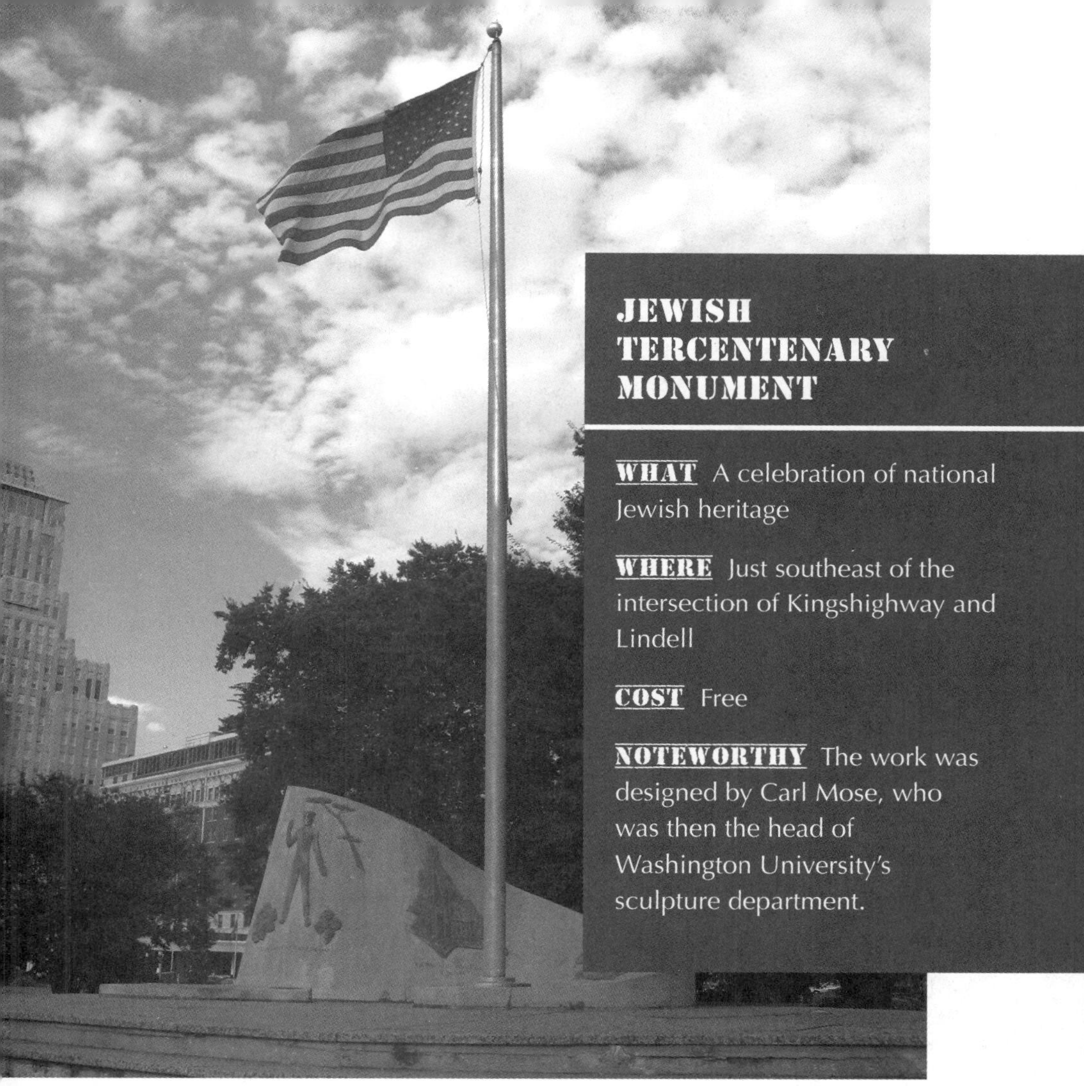

JEWISH TERCENTENARY MONUMENT

WHAT A celebration of national Jewish heritage

WHERE Just southeast of the intersection of Kingshighway and Lindell

COST Free

NOTEWORTHY The work was designed by Carl Mose, who was then the head of Washington University's sculpture department.

Many places around the nation marked the 300th anniversary of the arrival of the first Jews in America, but not all of them created a permanent physical reminder of the event.

As a side note, fountains along the edge of the plaza were a gift from the Koplar family, whose last name lent the famous call letters of St. Louis's own Channel 11—KPLR.

52 TORTOISE TIME

Why do concrete turtles dwell along Interstate 64?

Oakland Avenue may seem like your average block of charming brick apartment buildings punctuated with the occasional neighborhood tavern.

But one stretch of Oakland overlooks far more than just the buzzing traffic of Interstate 64. Cast a glance toward the highway, and you might be surprised to see one of the odder features found anywhere in the city.

Giant turtles.

The massive concrete tortoises include a hatchery and even a huge snake with its wide jaws clamped rather convincingly on a nearby Tamm Avenue bridge.

So what exactly is going on here?

This big fellow may not look friendly, but kids have enjoyed having their photos snapped in the mouth of this snapping turtle since its creation in 1996.

THE TURTLE PLAYGROUND

WHAT Tortoises without a hare in the world

WHERE Oakland and Tamm avenues

COST Free

PRO TIP In case this reptilian play place isn't enough for you, there is another turtle sculpture near the World's Fair Pavilion in Forest Park itself.

This unconventional landmark is actually the work of the equally unconventional Bob Cassilly, the eccentrically creative force behind City Museum.

Believing turtles to be symbolic of peace, philanthropist Sonya Glassberg backed the project financially. And today, St. Louis has one of the more unique landmarks found in any urban area.

The turtles aren't labeled at random. They are namesakes of donor Sonya Glassberg's family members.

What's in a name? A great deal along Oakland Avenue, where the concrete turtles are named after family of donor Sonya Glassberg. Meanwhile, the slithery border above representing a massive snake provides a distinctly non-traditional sight for drivers along Interstate 64. Children can also wander amongst cement turtle eggs in the little playground's hatchery.

53 JUST BARGE RIGHT IN

Where can you tour a working lock and dam system and operate a barge simulator?

No one fought harder to bring this engineering marvel into existence than the 21-term congressman whose name now graces its side, which makes it all the sadder that Melvin Price, who died in 1988, never got to see the final product of his political labors come into operation the following year.

Fortunately, you can. This exemplar of man's mastery over the mighty Mississippi is open at no cost for tourists with a hydrological bent.

Contrary to popular belief, the dam, which replaced the now dynamited Lock & Dam No. 26, has nothing to do with flood control. Rather, it is a vital part of the "9-foot channel project," a massive undertaking ensuring that the continent's most famous river would be navigable to barge traffic for its entire length.

Named for a Belleville congressman, the 1,160-foot-long dam contains two locks and is also home to the National Great Rivers Museum.

MELVIN PRICE LOCKS AND DAM

WHAT A crown jewel of river transport

WHERE 2 Locks & Dam Way, Alton, Ill.

COST Donations are appreciated

PRO TIP Tours leave at daily at 10 a.m., 1 p.m., and 3 p.m., and they aren't quick, lasting at least 45 minutes. Use the restroom beforehand.

And during your tour, you might indeed see a barge push through the lock. As much as a quarter-mile long, the widest craft run down the 110-foot-wide concrete passage with such hair-raising lack of clearance on either side, you'll be tempted to ask the tour guide dumb questions about whether it is bad if they scrape the edges. (Answer: Yes.)

Inside the affiliated National Great Rivers Museum, you can learn more about the workings of the dam and the river's history and even simulate the challenge of steering a barge through the narrow lock or—if you are like me—the challenge of embarrassingly ramming your simulated barge into it.

In 1990, its first full year of operation, the lock system carried more than 80 million tons of goods on barges.

If you tire of watching the real thing (top left), you can always get behind the controls of a simulated barge (top right). Your tour of the facility will also include a look at the high-water mark of the infamous 1993 flood, during which the locks remained open. Whatever you decide to do, don't miss the exhibits in the National Great Rivers Museum itself, which can relate the history of the Upper Mississippi and the vital role it still plays in transport.

54 FIVE BORDERS IN 45 SECONDS

How many municipalities can you drive through in less than a minute?

If you live in the Greater St. Louis area, you already know the answer is "a lot."

But if you find yourself on a certain stretch of Interstate 170, the answer becomes downright mind-boggling. One North County tract of the innerbelt crosses no less than five borders in less than three-quarters of a mile. Incredibly, part of this motoring adventure will have you pass through three city limits in a single tenth of a mile as you cross from Overland to Charlack to Sycamore Hills and back to Charlack again. That's just before you enter St. John on the south side of the St. Charles Rock Road exit and then hit Bel-Ridge on the opposite end of the overpass.

St. Louis County contains 90 municipalities as of 2015.

MUNICIPAL MADNESS

WHAT Cities, cities, everywhere

WHERE I-170 between Page Avenue and Natural Bridge Road

COST Metropolitan unity

PRO TIP A word to the wise—watch for speed traps.

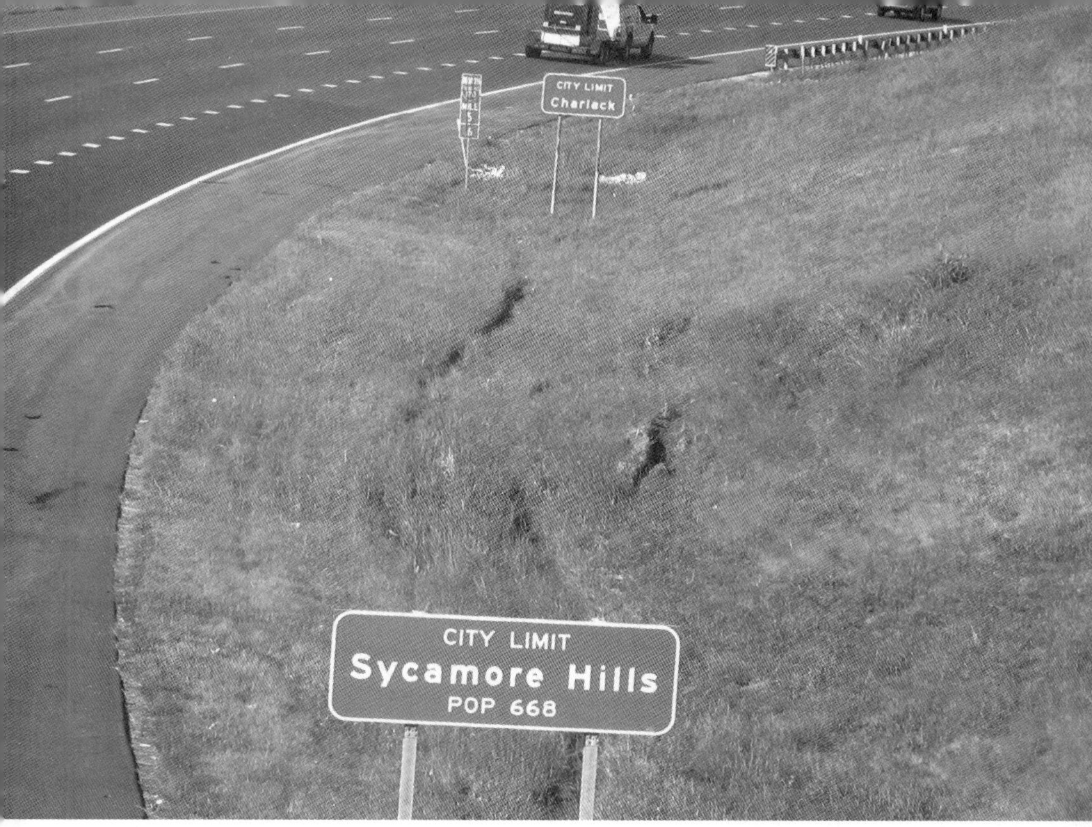

St. Louis's famously fractured geography is on full display in this bizarre section of Interstate 170 just north of Page Avenue.

You've just traveled through five cities—one of them twice—in well under 60 seconds. At times, as many as three different city limit signs are visible at the same time.

As comical as this might be, it also illustrates an important issue related to the municipal fragmentation that has long plagued our area. In few places is the difficulty laid out more starkly than here, an oddity that shows just how sadly estranged by parochialism our metropolitan area continues to be.

55 ABE LINCOLN'S SWORDFIGHT

Did "Honest Abe" nearly kill a man in the St. Louis area?

The Lincoln-Shields Recreation Area may be named for President Abraham Lincoln and one-time political opponent James Shields, but when the pair met in the vicinity in September 1842, their purposes were anything but recreational.

They were there to murder each other with swords.

In our nation's early days, dueling was often considered a tidy way to settle political disputes, but few realize that the man on the five-dollar bill, famous for his mellow personality, almost wound up in one. A young politician at the time, he was challenged to honorable combat after penning a series of satirical letters targeting Shields, Illinois's state auditor at the time, who found them considerably less humorous than their author. Sources vary

---

The Lincoln-Shields site is also the location of the former Lock & Dam No. 26, part of which is still there.

THE LINCOLN-SHIELDS RECREATION AREA

WHAT Lincoln's duel

WHERE Just west of U.S. 67 before the Clark Bridge

COST Free

PRO TIP For a treat, cross the river to Alton itself, which is chock full of history for Lincoln lovers.

A platform from the old Lock & Dam No. 26 provides a fine view of the City of Alton and is likely near where our 16th president nearly fought a duel, although no marker exists for the site.

on exactly where the two met to settle their differences, but most put it in the region of the spot near West Alton, Missouri, that now bears their names.

By most accounts, Lincoln had no desire to harm Shields and even less to die by his hand. The future president chose the unusual weapon of sabers, in which his height would give him an overwhelming advantage, and he hoped this would soften Shields' urge to fight. Eventually, it worked. Acquaintances mollified Shields and ultimately the potentially fatal encounter was called off. In later life, the pair even became friends.

Lincoln, for his part, seems to have been uncomfortable with the whole episode. In later life, he told one inquirer that he didn't deny the event but noted, "If you desire my friendship you will never mention it again."

56 ERUDITION ALONG THE BACK NINE

Why is the UM-St. Louis campus so hilly?

As any veteran UMSL student or alumnus knows, the physical education credits offered in classes aren't the only way you can get a workout at the University of Missouri. Any walk across the North Campus is usually enough of a trek over hill and dale to work up a pretty good sweat.

But did you ever wonder where a university could acquire that much land in an urban area?

The truth is that all of those hills were just perfect for UMSL's original use. Before becoming an institution of higher learning, it was actually a golf course. Purchased in 1957 by the Normandy School District, the plot was initially called the Normandy Residence Center.

The idea wasn't to form a university at all but simply a junior college to combat the Normandy district's low college entrance rate.

While some of UMSL's topography has changed, aspects of the original golf course remain. The unusually named Bugg Lake, honoring James Bugg, the university's first chancellor, is a former swimming hole for country club members. But according to a 1989 article in the student newspaper, there was some doubt as to whether the lake

---

UMSL counts two Fortune 20 CEOs among its 88,000 graduates worldwide.

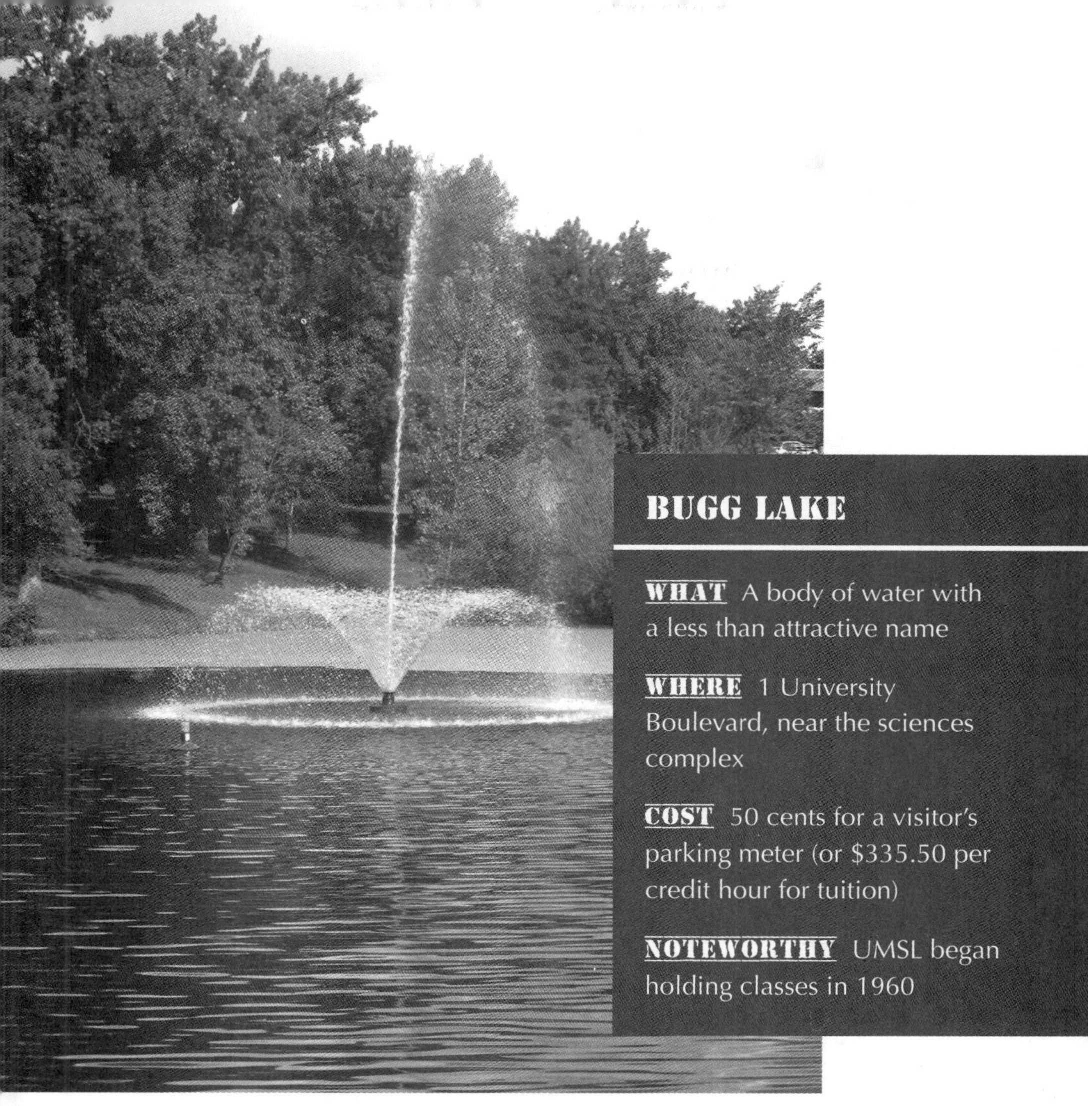

BUGG LAKE

WHAT A body of water with a less than attractive name

WHERE 1 University Boulevard, near the sciences complex

COST 50 cents for a visitor's parking meter (or $335.50 per credit hour for tuition)

NOTEWORTHY UMSL began holding classes in 1960

Bugg Lake isn't named for mosquitoes, but rather for a former chancellor of the school. Yet the body of water, along with the school's rolling hills, predates the campus and still speaks to its longtime history as a golf course.

actually had an official label at all. As for Bugg himself, the chancellor hadn't really wanted the pond named after him in the first place, finally conceding "but if the students want to call it that, it is sure alright with me."

57 THINK LOCALLY, LABEL GLOBALLY

How did this area of North County get such an odd name?

Let's start with the obvious. There's something just a bit weird about the cosmic-sounding moniker of this business park in northwest St. Louis County hugging the Missouri River.

Earth City?

For starters, there is the obvious contradiction: Earth City isn't a planet.

Yet it also isn't a city. There are no borders, mayor or, for that matter, residents. It is impossible to motor through this attractive complex of tidy offices and well-manicured corporate lawns without wondering where exactly it got this odd name. Were the original buildings made of dirt? Was the land plotted between Venus Town and Mars Village?

Developers originally planned a nine-hole golf course for Earth City but it never came to be.

EARTH CITY

WHAT A little business park with a very big name

WHERE Northwest St. Louis County (along the Earth City Expressway, of course)

COST Free

NOTEWORTHY The business park is protected from the Missouri River's ravages by a 500-year levee.

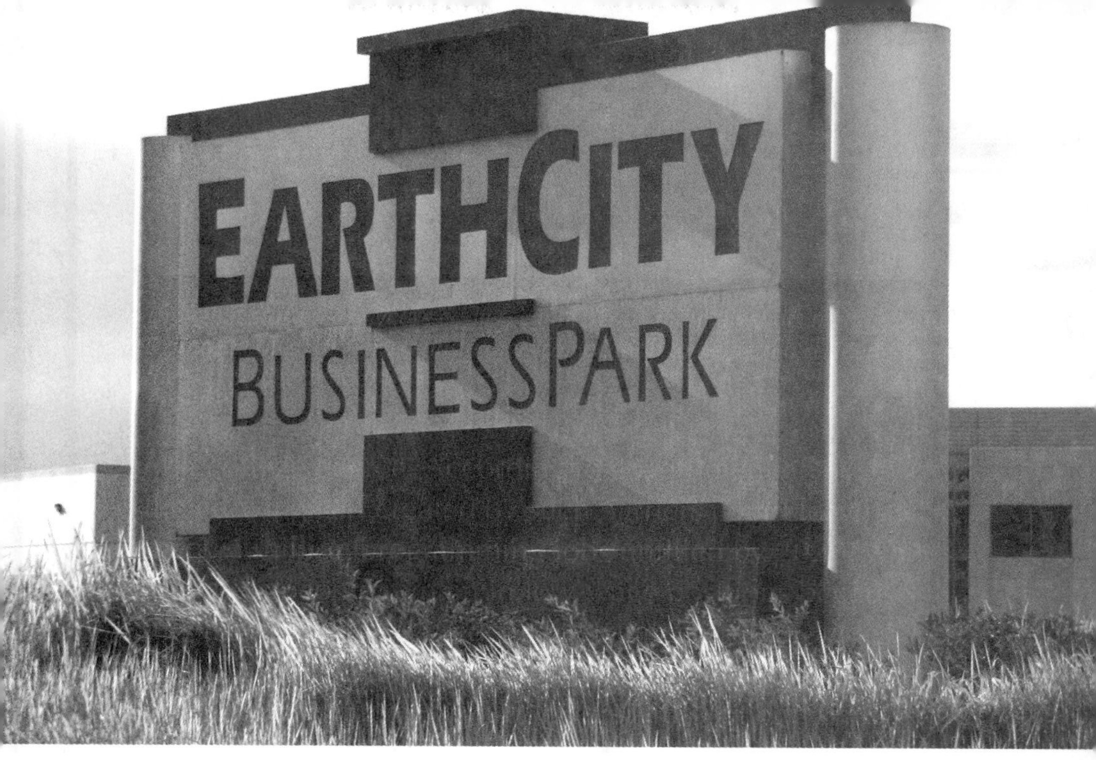

You may need directions to this business park, but at least you know what part of the solar system to start in.

The reality is more mundane. When the original developers organized the business park in 1971, "earth" was a huge buzzword. Earth Day had just been established the preceding year, and hippie culture had infused ecological terminology into the nation's cultural bloodstream. As for the "city" part, it turns out that planners initially envisioned more than 4,000 rental units. Earth City was supposed to have residents. That idea had faded by the early 1980s, but the appellation "city" stuck. So did the business park's unique planetary name, despite the development's management exploring the idea of a change to a less unusual moniker at one point.

However, ultimately, they chose not to mess with what worked. Earth City is a bustling success so Earth City is what it remains to this day.

58 LORD OF THE RIVERS: THE TWO TOWERS

What on earth are those weird little castles doing in the middle of the river?

Almost anyone who has crossed the Mississippi on Interstate 270's bridge at Chain of Rocks has probably wondered about them at one time or another. Two strange castle-like objects rise from the river on the bridge's south side. Without discernible reason, they stand as though transported from a fairy tale into the heart of a major American waterway. Just what are they doing there?

In fact, the two odd structures are intake stations for the city's water department. Known by the fairly mundane labels "Intake Tower 1" and "Intake Tower 2," the pair of little castles did indeed serve a pretty exciting functional role in the city's history by helping to bring fresh water to St. Louisans and lessening worry over such diseases as cholera in the area. The older of the pair came online in the 1890s, with its sister joining it a couple decades later.

If they seem just a bit too decorative for plumbing facilities, you shouldn't underestimate the aesthetic value of good solid hydrological infrastructure. After all, the

---

The intake stations are not open to the public and the waters around them are pretty tricky, so they can only be viewed from afar.

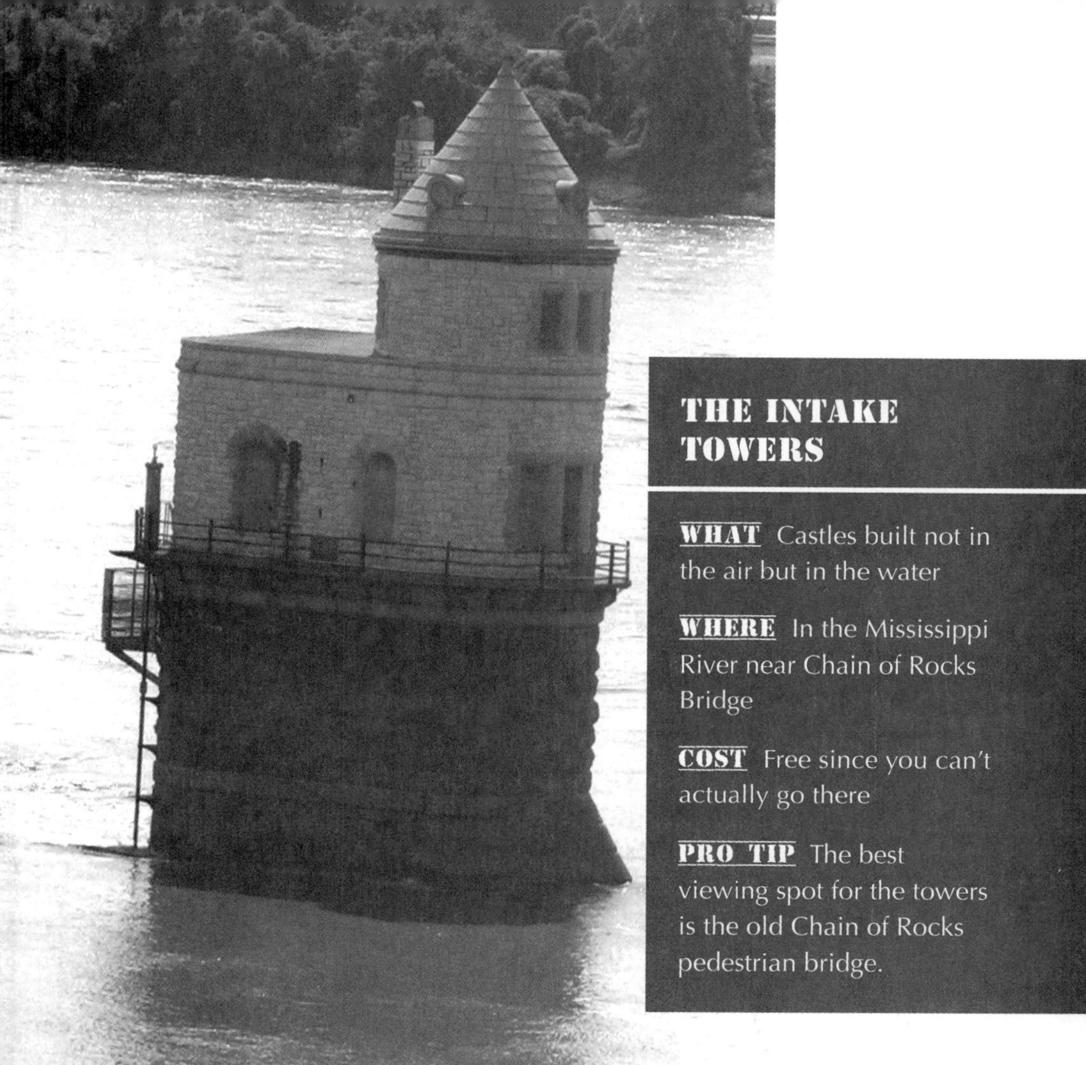

THE INTAKE TOWERS

WHAT Castles built not in the air but in the water

WHERE In the Mississippi River near Chain of Rocks Bridge

COST Free since you can't actually go there

PRO TIP The best viewing spot for the towers is the old Chain of Rocks pedestrian bridge.

Intake Tower Number 1 takes St. Louisans back to a time when clean drinking water must have seemed almost as exotic as a castle in the middle of a river.

distinctive design of the White Castle fast food restaurants was in fact inspired by a Chicago water tower.

The Mississippi River structures don't see a ton of visitors these days, but the little castles are far more than just a river curiosity for baffled motorists traversing between Illinois and Missouri. They are a vital part of our past.

59 THE GENTLE GIANT

Where can you pay respects to the world's tallest man?

By their very nature, statues make some men seem larger than life. But for the memorial honoring Robert Wadlow, that was never a problem. At 8′ 11″, Wadlow holds the record as the tallest human being ever confirmed to exist, and the St. Louis area can proudly claim him as a native.

A resident of Alton, Illinois, Wadlow was born in 1918 with no particularly distinguishing physical characteristics. But quickly, that began to change. Thanks to a pituitary condition, Wadlow was already wearing clothing meant for teenagers by the time he entered kindergarten and he stood taller than most grown men by age 10.

Wadlow was famous for his good nature, becoming known as "The Gentle Giant." And his stature brought him a degree of fame and the opportunity to travel. He logged tens of thousands of miles on the road touring for the International Shoe Company, which provided his size 37 footwear. He was able to fit in the car for the trip only through removal of the front seat.

But Wadlow's height presented any number of physical challenges as well, and he needed more than just special shoes. The plaza with his statue in Alton includes a replica of the custom chair built for him, which required 11 yards of fabric to cover.

For his 15th birthday, Wadlow received a card measuring more than 300 square feet.

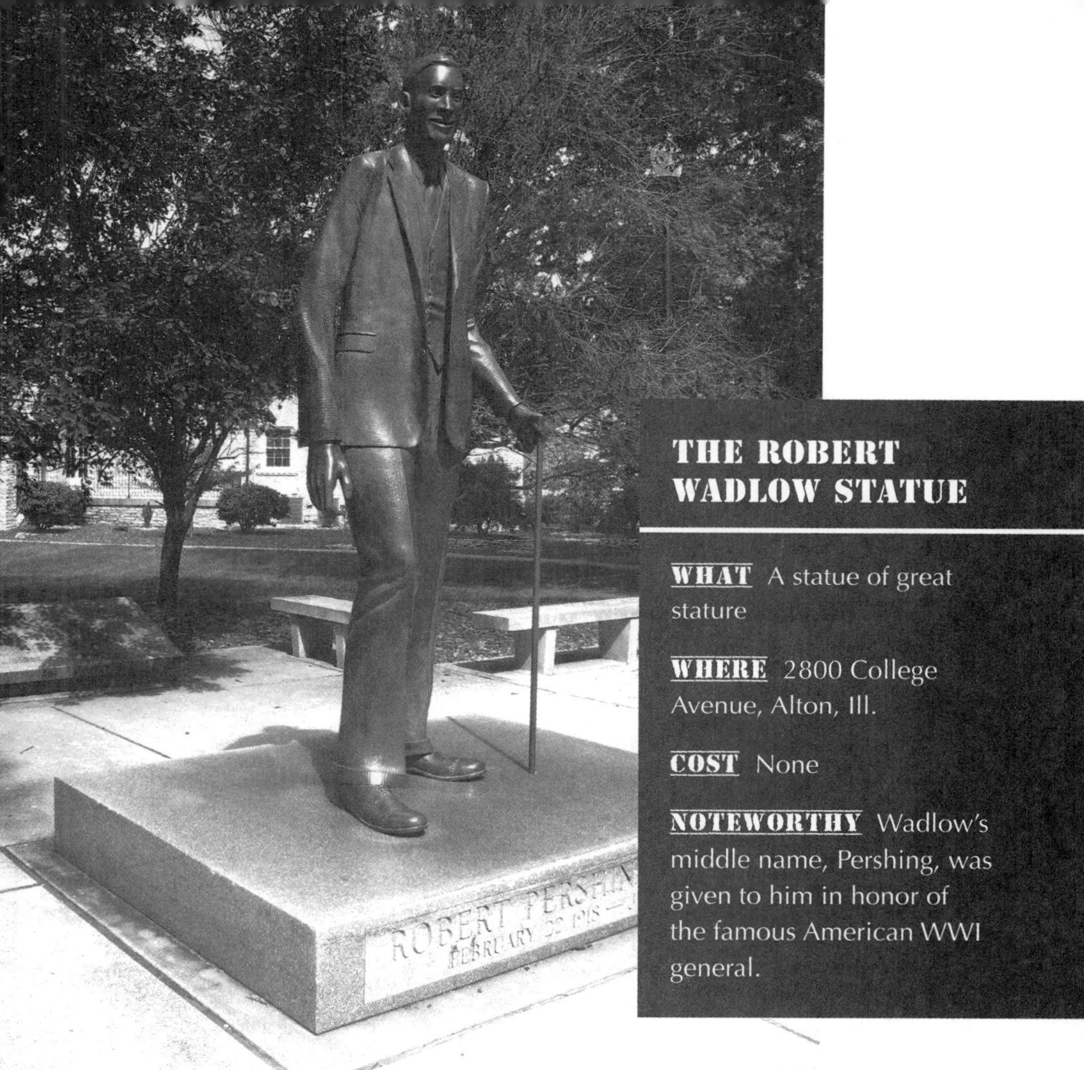

Robert Wadlow was known as much for his noble heart as for his notable height.

THE ROBERT WADLOW STATUE

WHAT A statue of great stature

WHERE 2800 College Avenue, Alton, Ill.

COST None

NOTEWORTHY Wadlow's middle name, Pershing, was given to him in honor of the famous American WWI general.

Unfortunately, the condition that brought Wadlow notoriety also resulted in his untimely demise. Numbness in his feet contributed to the development of a blister and infection that rapidly advanced, ending his extraordinary life less than five years after high school graduation.

60 TAKING FLIGHT

Where can you see a drone that has flown in Afghanistan?

What's past is prologue, as Shakespeare once wrote, but at Boeing, that's exactly where the past is supposed to be.

The aerospace giant's James S. McDonnell Prologue Room is dedicated to storing and displaying a wide array of materials chronicling the history of Boeing and the companies with which it joined over the years, particularly the heritage of McDonnell Douglas, the longtime contractor headquartered in St. Louis.

Exhibits on display include representations of numerous military and civilian aircraft, as well as space capsules from the Gemini and Mercury programs, which engineers on earth used as test pieces. Models of planes ranging from the F-15 Eagle fighter to Air Force One adorn walls, ceilings, and glass cases. Information about pioneers and corporate leaders are shown as well.

Fans of flight history will be in heaven at the Prologue Room, which sometimes seems like it has everything short of the Wright Brothers' first test plane.

THE McDONNELL PROLOGUE ROOM

WHAT The history of aerospace

WHERE Building 100 at Boeing on Airport Road next to Lambert

COST Free

PRO TIP Guided tours for groups of 10 or more are available year round with a reservation, but if you'd just like to stop by and look around by yourself, Prologue is only open June–August.

And, yes, there is even an actual surveillance drone that once flew missions in Afghanistan and is now enjoying its retirement as a showpiece.

Announced in 1996, the merger between Boeing and McDonnell Douglas created a company with annual revenue estimated at $48 billion.

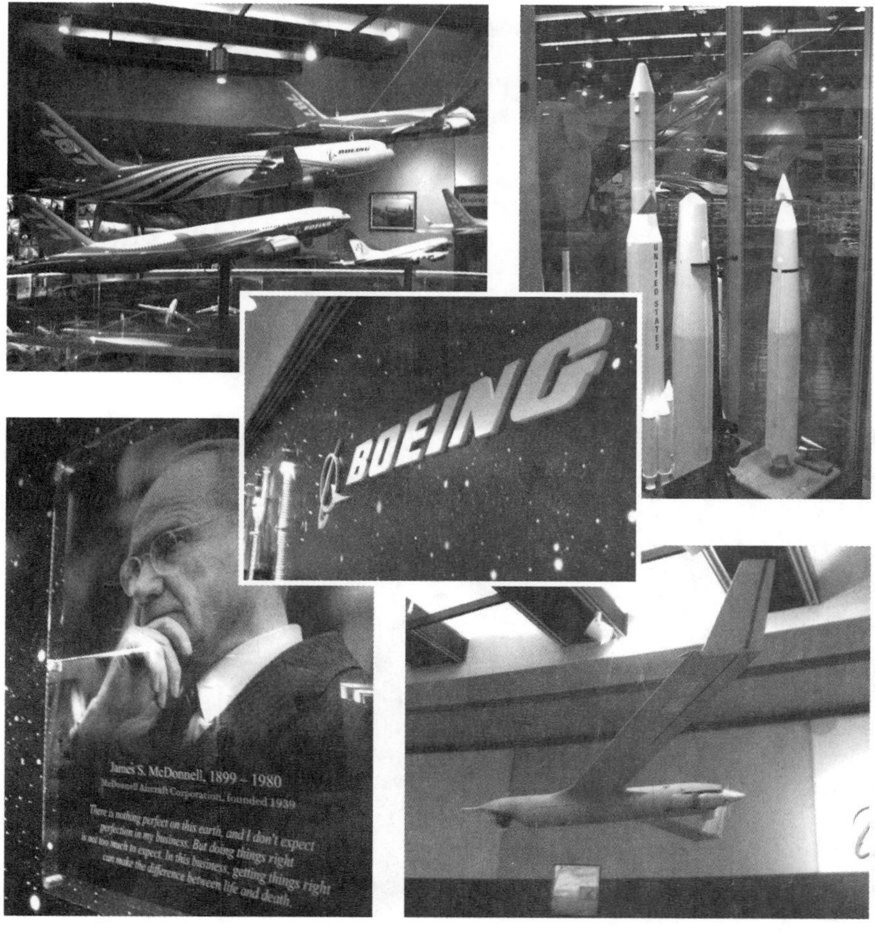

Looking a bit like a hobbyist's dream world, scale models, mock-ups, and even a few actual working vehicles festoon virtually every surface and bit of floor space at the James S. McDonnell Prologue Room, where missile technology, commercial aircraft, and rocketry advances provide a feast for the aerospace enthusiast in all of us.

61 CONFLUENCE–EAST

Where can you see Edwardsville and Clayton at the same time?

It's a tall order—literally—but you can indeed view both the SIUE campus and the glass and concrete edifices of St. Louis County's seat of government from the same spot, even though the two are a solid 40-minute drive from each other. That spot is the Lewis and Clark Confluence Tower near the meeting of the Missouri and Mississippi rivers in Hartford, Illinois.

But this 180-foot tower with three viewing platforms enlightens as well as elevates. The structure's visitors' center at its base gives a broad overview of the region's topography. Meanwhile, each level expands the physical view of the area while sharing information about various parts of the panorama the visitor experiences, beginning

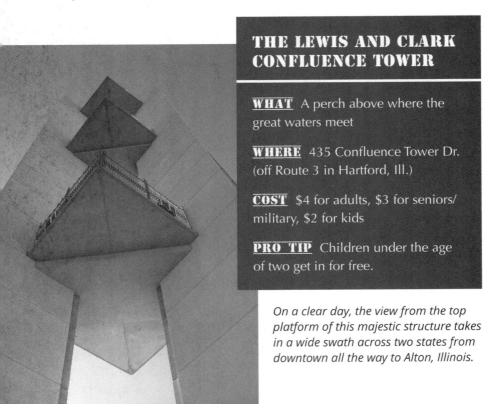

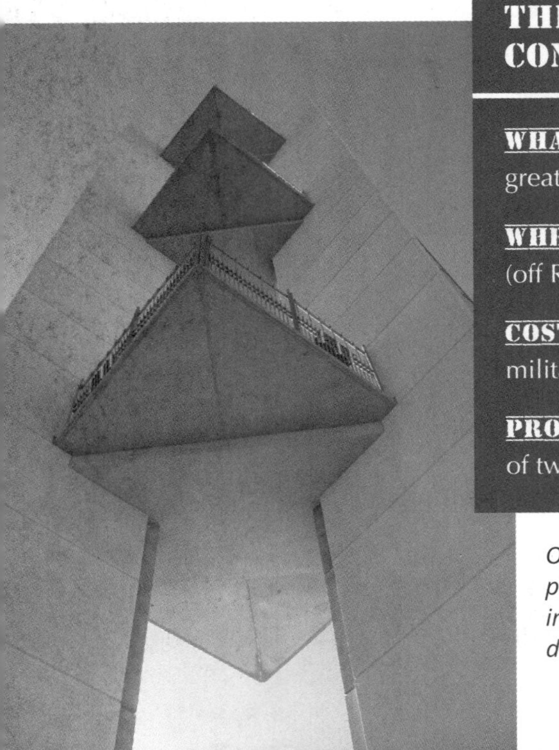

THE LEWIS AND CLARK CONFLUENCE TOWER

WHAT A perch above where the great waters meet

WHERE 435 Confluence Tower Dr. (off Route 3 in Hartford, Ill.)

COST $4 for adults, $3 for seniors/military, $2 for kids

PRO TIP Children under the age of two get in for free.

On a clear day, the view from the top platform of this majestic structure takes in a wide swath across two states from downtown all the way to Alton, Illinois.

with the development of Hartford and continuing with an explanation of the Meeting of the Great Rivers National Scenic Byway.

The tower, which opened in 2010, is open Wednesday through Sunday.

The Confluence Tower contains more than 2,000 truckloads of concrete.

Weather permitting, you can indeed see the Gateway Arch in downtown, though the Arch is about three-and-a-half times taller, so it is probably doing more of the work. Meanwhile, check out the exhibits in the visitors' center and learn more about Lewis and Clark, the duo that the confluence structure honors.

62 CONFLUENCE–WEST

What is the easternmost point of St. Louis County?

All good things must come to an end—even the beauty of St. Louis County. And after motoring a winding, nearly five-mile course across the undeveloped swamps and grasslands in the northern bulge of land below the Missouri River, you'll be there. Columbia Bottom Conservation Area is essentially the furthest east you can get and still be in the cozy confines of the county. A concrete viewing platform overlooks the merging of the continent's two mightiest waterways, allowing for a moment's reflection upon what it really means to live in the center of America.

Of course, when you are west of the Mississippi, there is more than one option for seeing the famous confluence of the rivers. In St. Louis County, Columbia Bottom offers the fullest vantage point from a bluff, adding a degree of height

COLUMBIA BOTTOM CONSERVATION AREA

WHAT Land's end for St. Louis Countians

WHERE Columbia Bottom at the termination of Upper Columbia Bottom Road

COST Free

PRO TIP Fowl hunting is permitted but consult state conservation department rules at https://extra.mdc.mo.gov/documents/area_brochures/9736.pdf for details

This Columbia Bottom viewing platform in St. Louis County showcases the meeting of the Missouri and Mississippi rivers. On the far left is St. Charles County. The more distant shore to the right is Illinois. In the middle is every drop of water from any creek, brook, or stream from Minnesota to Montana.

to the experience. Still, if you insist on communing directly with the rivers at water level, then Edward "Ted" and Pat Jones Confluence State Park on the St. Charles County side may be the better option. Be aware though that the Jones experience will include a slow, dusty 4.7-mile trek along a remarkably unpaved road.

And that's if Jones is open at all, which, due to its position at what is essentially one of the most floodable points on Planet Earth, it frequently isn't.

At more than 3,700 miles, the Mississippi-Missouri river system is the fourth longest in the world behind the Nile, Amazon, and Yangtze.

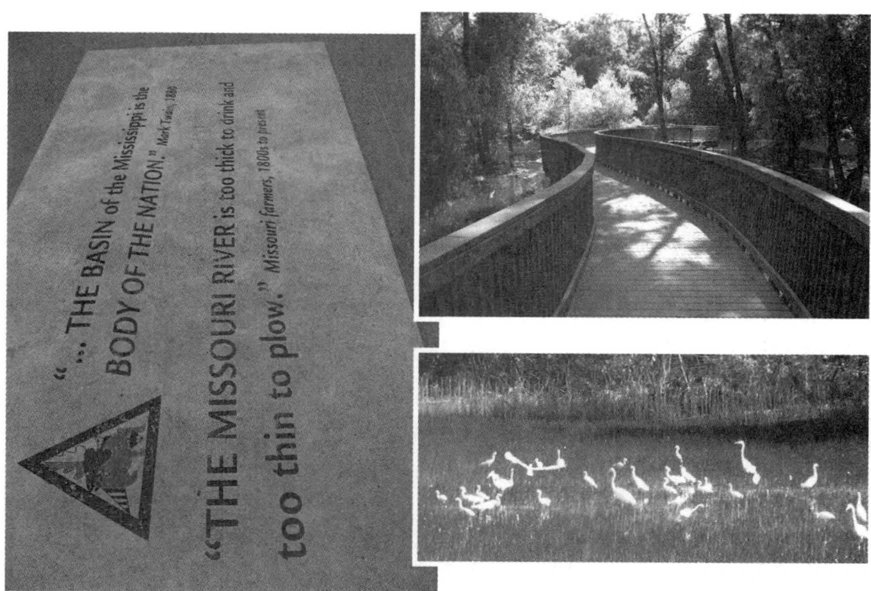

When it comes to taking in the confluence, Columbia Bottom has a distinct advantage over the other two viewing locations in Hartford, Illinois, and Jones Park in St. Charles County—namely, that the drive out there is just as awesome as the destination. Waterfowl abound throughout the conservation area as do frogs and other wildlife. A special turnout parking lot allows for visitation of a walkway through the wetlands to view turtles and fish swimming wild in the murky water.

63 THE BOOTS OF O'FALLON, MO

What does this empty footwear represent in a local St. Charles County suburb?

They stand in eternal vigilance. They stand at silent attention. They stand in the place of brothers, sisters, sons, and daughters who, in some cases, are no longer there to wear them.

At first, this plaza of disembodied bronze footwear may cause a passerby to do a double take, but quickly the Veterans Memorial Walk of O'Fallon, Missouri, brings home a message as simple and direct as it is powerful and personal. Dedicated in 2001, just as America found itself on the brink of two military conflicts, the five rows

In 2015, the Military Times honored O'Fallon as one of the best places in the nation for veterans to live.

VETERANS MEMORIAL WALK

WHAT Boots with a message

WHERE 800 Belleau Creek Road, in O'Fallon, MO

COST None

PRO TIP Ceremonies are held here on Veterans and Memorial Days as well as Armed Forces and POW/MIA Remembrance Days.

Honoring all American soldiers, these pairs of boots are each positioned with one slightly in front of the other to suggest the concept of a forward march by a unit of men and women in uniform.

of empty boots, each decorated tastefully with a ribbon of remembrance, sit in front of five markers representing the different uniformed services, while a flame is kept continuously burning on a pedestal.

Nearby, one pair of boots by itself represents POWs and those missing in action whose fate sometimes remains a mystery for years after a conflict's end.

64 THE STAR OF O'FALLON, IL

What does this star-shaped memorial in a Metro East neighborhood mean?

Veterans have an honored place on the east end of the St. Louis area as well as the west, and the City of O'Fallon, Illinois, is no less innovative than its similarly named Missouri cousin in the means by which it recognizes those who have served.

When seen from the ground, these rows of engraved stone pillars with words like "liberty," "sacrifice," "duty," and "allegiance" situated next to a peaceful lake are beautiful enough, but when seen from above, a whole new level of meaning becomes apparent. The concrete walkways form a perfect star.

O'FALLON VETERANS MONUMENT

WHAT A star of honor

WHERE 737 E. Wesley Drive

COST None to visit

PRO TIP Use the on-site electronic kiosk to find a particular vet's name and location.

During evening hours, the monument is kept brightened by artificial lighting.

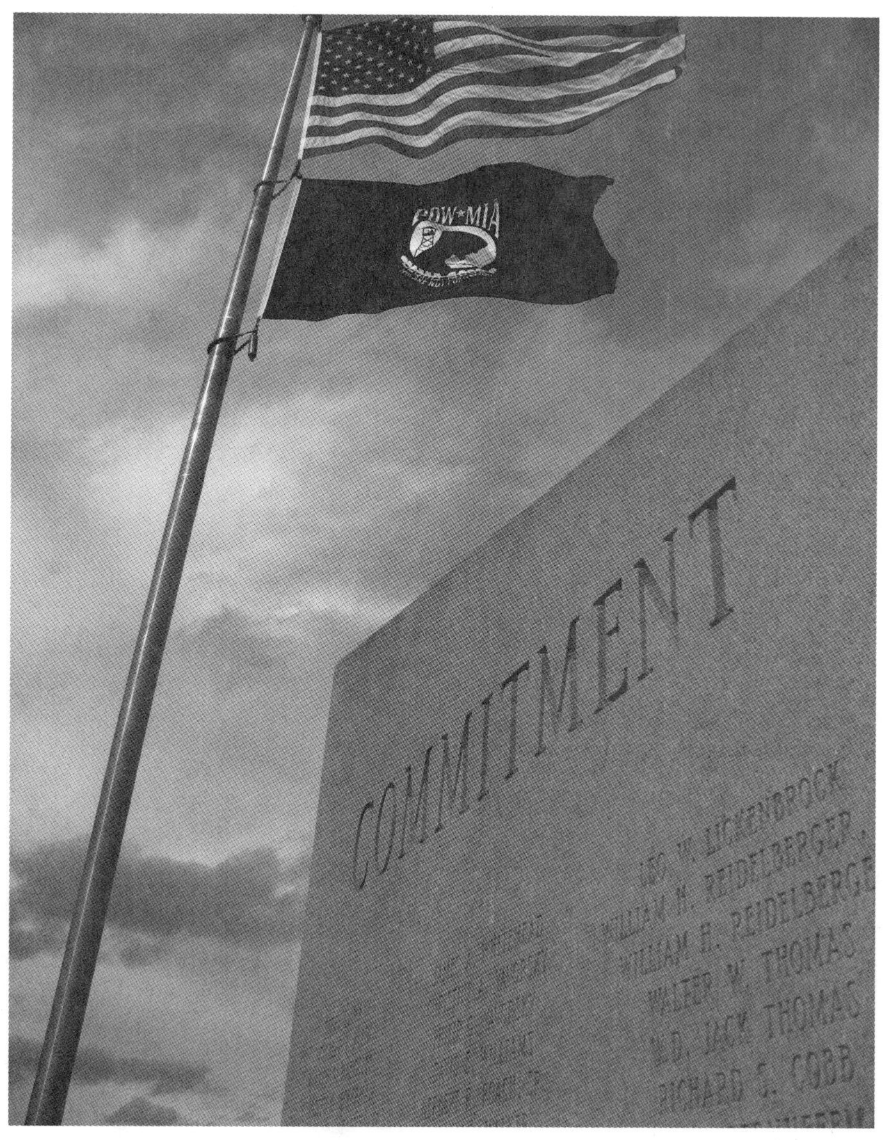

The monument's pillars contain names from the Army, Navy, Air Force, Marines, and Coast Guard.

The more than 1,700 names represent honorably discharged veterans from O'Fallon Township or its associated school district.

New entries are engraved twice a year with names appearing by Veterans or Memorial days.

65 THE GREAT DEBATE

Did one of America's most famous debates happen here?

Many would say that our nation has become too accustomed to the heavily stage-managed nature of modern political dialogue. What was once a contest of ideas or a battle of principles often seems now more a lifeless bit of well-practiced theater dominated by glib one-liners and an obsession over gaffes.

But in 1858, when challenger Abraham Lincoln took on incumbent Stephen Douglas for a U.S. Senate seat, the pair staged a series of debates staking out positions that helped define the national divide just two years before the

Unlike the sound bite-friendly, televised, back-and-forth debates of modernity, Lincoln and Douglas gave lengthy speeches lasting up to 90 minutes at a time. Imagine trying to put that on CNN or YouTube.

LINCOLN-DOUGLAS SQUARE

WHAT A debate for the ages

WHERE Downtown Alton

COST None

NOTEWORTHY About 6,000 people attended the debate, although newspapers carried its message much farther.

Douglas prevailed in the election, but the debate immortalized here would ultimately cost more than half-a-million American lives to resolve on battlefields from Shiloh to Gettysburg.

outbreak of civil war. The last of those seven meetings took place in Alton, Illinois, and is commemorated today with statues of the pair—a tall, thin Lincoln deep in thought as the portlier Douglas punches the air with his finger to make a point while the two battled over issues of slavery and states' rights.

When Democrats took control of the state legislature, their nominee Douglas won the election. But it was Lincoln who effectively won the argument, later defeating his old opponent for president in 1860, and it was Lincoln who would go down in history as having taken the side of human freedom over cruel bondage.

66 COLOSSAL CONDIMENT OF COLLINSVILLE

Where can you find the world's largest ketchup bottle?

They say that every town has a claim to fame—some perhaps a bit stranger than others.

But for folks in Collinsville, Illinois, staking a planetwide claim to the biggest ketchup bottle is something residents are quite proud of. The 70-foot-tall condiment container perched atop a 100-foot tower along Route 159 even has its own fan page on the Internet, and when it needed repainting and revamping in the 1990s, donors got on board to return it to its former glory. There's even an annual festival to celebrate the big bottle, complete with hot dog- and tater tot-eating contests.

The "bottle" of course, is actually a water tower constructed to promote Brooks brand ketchup. Completed in 1949, the huge tank is emblazoned with the company logo. The Brooks name, once a remarkably big player in the tomato condiment business, is now owned by Birds Eye Foods, which does still make the ketchup but only for what the bottle's website describes as "very limited distribution."

Ketchup is originally a Chinese invention; however, the initial version was fish-based and did not involve tomatoes.

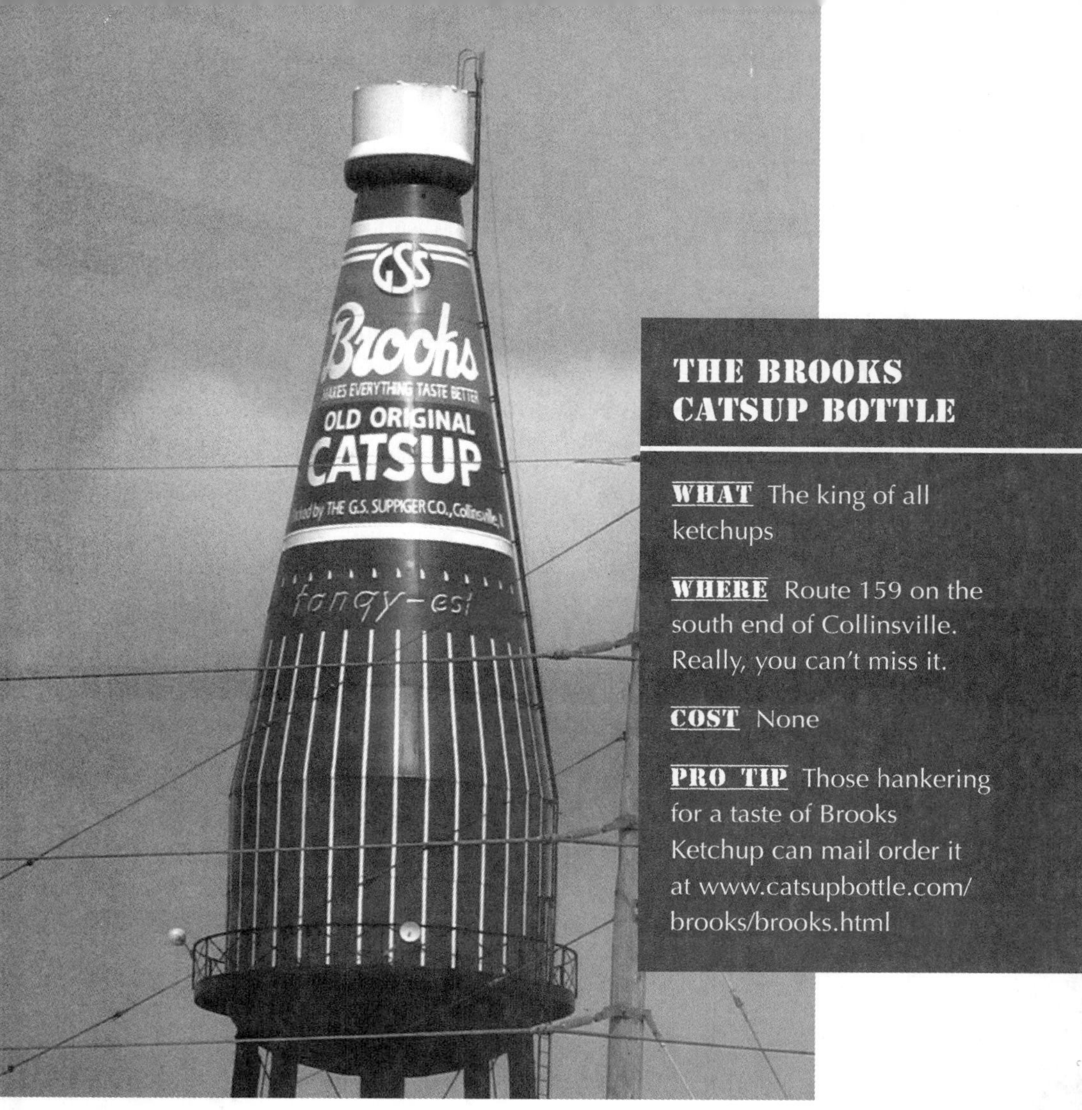

THE BROOKS CATSUP BOTTLE

WHAT The king of all ketchups

WHERE Route 159 on the south end of Collinsville. Really, you can't miss it.

COST None

PRO TIP Those hankering for a taste of Brooks Ketchup can mail order it at www.catsupbottle.com/brooks/brooks.html

Brooks now renders its ketchup with a "K," but sometimes only the classical spelling will do.

In 2002, the tower, which hasn't been owned by Brooks' successor companies since 1993, attained a spot on the National Register of Historic Places.

67 RESPECT FOR ROVER

Where can you find the canine hall of fame?

Sure, we call him man's best friend, but when the chips are down, when do we ever give our furry buddies more than canned food and an occasional belly rub?

Well, at the American Kennel Club's Museum of the Dog, canines are king. Established in 1981 as The Dog Museum of America, the institution would move from New York City to St. Louis later in the decade and today encompasses more than 14,000 square feet, much of it dedicated to portraits and ceramics of various dog breeds and such unusual items as a Palladian-style dog house that looks more ornate than where most of us humans probably call home.

The real treat is downstairs, where famous pooches from Lassie to Toto reside in the doggie Hall of Fame. However, canines with more serious occupations are seen here

AKC'S MUSEUM OF THE DOG

WHAT Fame for fortunate Fidos

WHERE 1721 South Mason Road

COST $5 for adults, $2.50 for seniors/military, $1 for children

PRO TIP Don't neglect the architecture. Built in 1853, the Jarville House is a marvel of the Greek Revival school and was once owned by Monsanto's Edgar Queeny, for whom the surrounding park is now named.

This majestic fellow stands guard in the county's most hallowed grounds of dogdom between two stately flags. Among many notable show dogs, those featured in the Hall of Fame include movie star Rin Tin Tin and the "Beagle Brigade," which helps the U.S. Department of Agriculture sniff out banned plant and food items at American ports of entry.

as well, including search-and-rescue animals from the Oklahoma City bombing and 9/11 attacks. A different exhibit deals with dogs in wartime, and there's even a special police dog wall for St. Louis County's four-footed finest to pose with their badges on.

And, before you ask, yes, dogs are allowed at the facility through a "Fido-friendly" visitation policy as long as they are leashed and obedience-trained. Consult www.museumofthedog.org for details.

Terry, the dog who played Toto in *The Wizard of Oz*, was called "he" in the film but was actually a female.

A portrait of former White House dog Millie sits next to a framed letter from then-First Lady Barbara Bush.

Portraiture is a big part of the museum, but many ceramics and even movie posters, like the one at right, can be found. Alas, there are no iconic "dogs playing poker" paintings, but we can't expect everything.

68 THE OTHER ST. LOUIS ARCH

Do we have more than one noteworthy bit of "arch"itecture?

For better or worse, St. Louis was fated to be defined by the shape of an arch from the moment its most famous example of one opened downtown in 1965.

But the Gateway to the West has another arch of note just a few blocks away—and this one is quite a bit older and has abilities that even its big brother on the riverfront lacks. Bargain-hunters at Union Station can punctuate their visits to the shopping venue's many stores and eateries with a trip to the Whispering Arch, an entryway to the Grand Hall

---

German architect Theodore Link, who has now been recognized on the St. Louis Walk of Fame, designed Union Station in 1894.

UNION STATION WHISPERING ARCH

WHAT A locale where disembodied voices are only a bit of science fun

WHERE St. Louis's beautiful Union Station at the entrance to the Grand Hall

COST None except for parking and the joys of shopping

NOTEWORTHY The last train to depart Union Station did so on Halloween 1978.

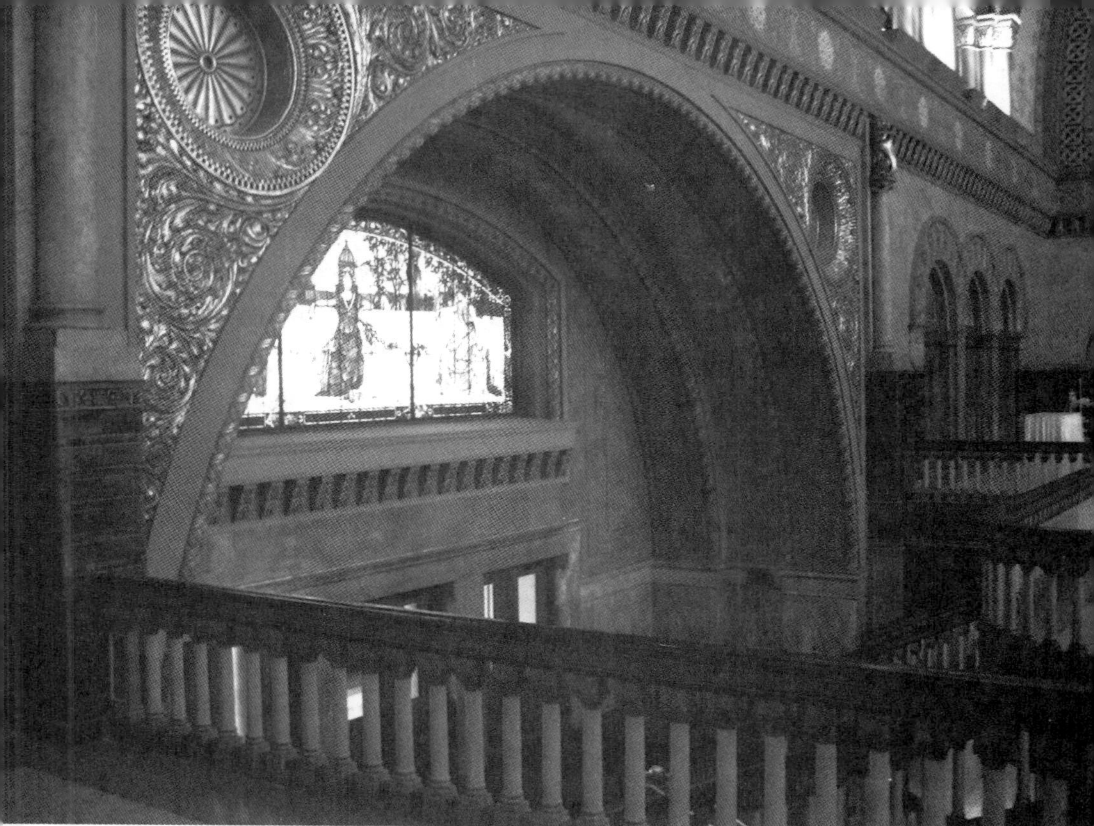

This arch may not have quite the imposing presence as the one run by the National Park Service, but its special acoustical properties still amuse visitors. Supposedly, the quirk was first noticed by a workman who accidentally dropped a hammer.

that allows a person at one leg to have their voice heard at the other leg 50 feet away. Curving like a rainbow above exquisite stained glass windows, the arch, like so much of the beautiful former train depot, is a work of art in and of itself.

The arch's acoustical oddity actually isn't that unusual. Whispering arches have been found in buildings the world over, including Union Station's New York cousin, Grand Central Station.

69 THE UNIVERSE IN A FEW EASY STEPS

Can you walk the whole solar system while never leaving the Delmar Loop?

Okay, so most of us won't make it out into space anytime soon, but that doesn't mean we can't learn a little more about our nearest celestial neighbors a bit closer to home. That's the idea behind St. Louis's Planetwalk.

Stretching just over half a mile from end to end, this series of signposts representing each of the planets will give you an idea of the vastness of the great beyond while not taking you too far from trendy shopping venues.

Erected in 2009, the attraction is a bit more abbreviated than the real solar system, but it can at least present a taste of what the scope of travel would be like to each

The scale for the Loop's Planetwalk is 5,000,000,000 to 1

THE PLANETWALK

WHAT The entire solar system

WHERE The Delmar Loop

COST Free

NOTEWORTHY Because it was built after the planetoid's 2006 demotion, the Delmar Loop Planetwalk does not include Pluto.

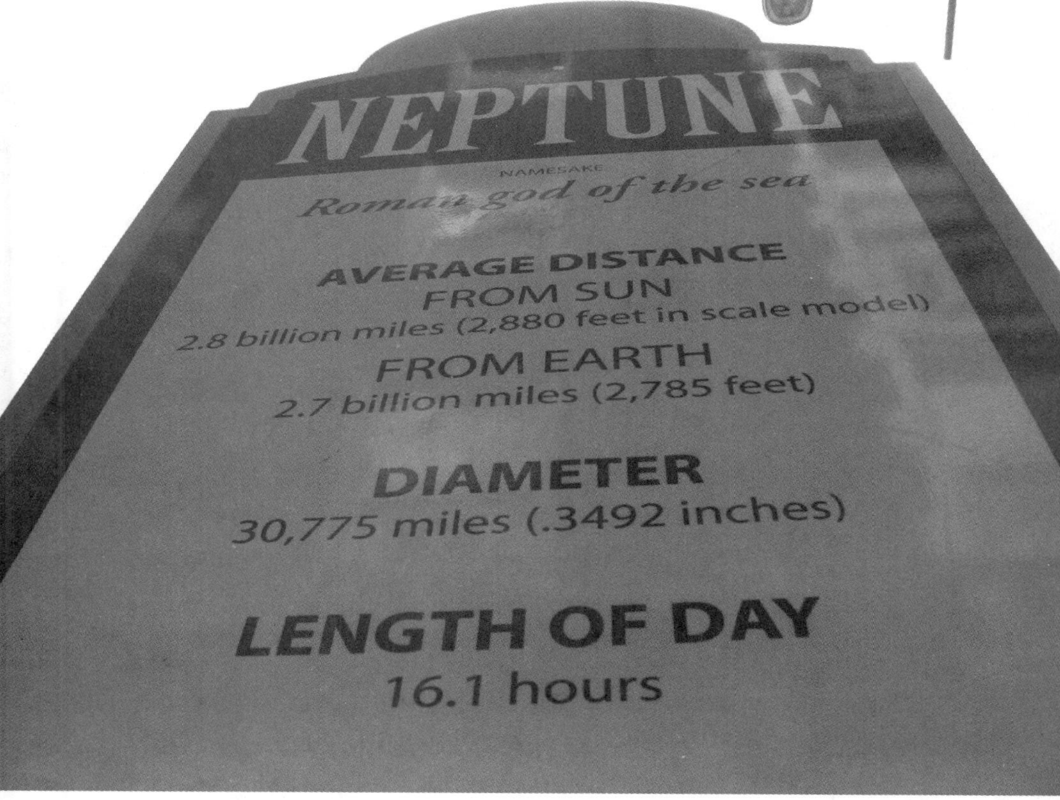

NEPTUNE
NAMESAKE
Roman god of the sea
AVERAGE DISTANCE
FROM SUN
2.8 billion miles (2,880 feet in scale model)
FROM EARTH
2.7 billion miles (2,785 feet)
DIAMETER
30,775 miles (.3492 inches)
LENGTH OF DAY
16.1 hours

Neptune is 2.7 billion miles from Earth but only 100 feet from great pizza and convenient parking.

celestial body—assuming you didn't lack good restaurants in between. Information on a given planet is provided by its plaque. A single inch of Delmar Boulevard on the Planetwalk is equal to roughly 80,000 miles in space terms, a ratio surprisingly close to the way drivers actually feel when caught in Loop traffic on a Saturday night.

The exhibit runs east to west, with Neptune positioned in front of Cicero's at Delmar and Kingsland and the sun positioned—ironically enough—in front of the Moonrise Hotel.

Travelers who start from the east should be aware that the walking gets a lot longer once you traverse past Mars and the inner solar system, which is small enough to be contained within a single block.

70 KIRKWOOD'S TRUE BREAD WINNER

Why is Panera called St. Louis Bread Company only in St. Louis?

Many things about St. Louis confuse out-of-towners. However, one of the most baffling anomalies may lie in the roots of Panera, a bakery that now has more than 1,900 locations across 46 states. Visitors may recognize the menu, the service, even the logo.

But the name may prompt a double take.

In all the cities where Panera exists, only the handful of its establishments near St. Louis are named after the metro area they inhabit. Only here is Panera referred to as the St. Louis Bread Company.

That's because the enterprise affectionately known to locals as "Bread Co." started right here in the Gateway City.

THE FORMER HOME OF THE FIRST ST. LOUIS BREAD COMPANY

WHAT A local name on a national company

WHERE 10312 Manchester Road in Kirkwood (now occupied by Winfield's Gathering Place)

COST Depends on how hungry you are

NOTEWORTHY The St. Louis Bread Company started on just $300,000.

The first St. Louis Bread Company began operations on October 19, 1987, the day of the infamous "Black Monday" stock market crash.

Today, a sports bar known as Winfield's Gathering Place has the spot in the 10300 block of Manchester where the first St. Louis Bread Company started in 1987. Winfield's, which took over the space in 2015, was opened with ex-Cardinal Jim Edmonds as a partner. The BBQ burnt ends sourdough melt is said to be a house specialty.

Inspired by cozy cafes he saw during a trip to San Francisco, the company was brought to life by a fellow named Ken Rosenthal in 1987. The idea turned out to be such a hit with patrons that it attracted the attention of Au Bon Pain, a significantly larger East Coast outfit in the same market space that finally laid out $23 million to purchase the little chain.

Yet the Bread Company concept turned out to be so successful that something very unusual happened. The parent company began imitating its child. Rechristened as Panera, the concept that had made 20 St. Louis-area outlets a success was tweaked for a national audience and began to grow faster than a leavened baguette. Amazingly, Au Bon Pain sold off its own stores to throw everything it could into Panera, which by 1999 became the moniker of the entire company. Today, Panera is a household name—except, of course, for a single city where the old label remains as a quiet tribute to where it was born.

The world has Panera. Only St. Louis has the St. Louis Bread Company.

Though the slot is now occupied by a different restaurant, you can still visit the location of the very first Bread Company in a Kirkwood shopping center along Manchester and see exactly where this Gateway City original was born.

71 MULTIPLE McKINLEYS

Who is this bridge really named after?

Named for President William McKinley, this gritty-looking span has carried car traffic just north of downtown for decades. It has just two oddities. It isn't named for President William McKinley, and its primary purpose wasn't to carry car traffic.

Well, strictly speaking, it was named for a President William McKinley. It just isn't the President William McKinley you are thinking of. The William McKinley who gave the bridge its name was in fact president of the Illinois Electric Traction Association. In other words, he's the fellow who made the trains run on time.

In 2015, Alaska's Mt. McKinley, the continent's highest peak – which really was named for the U.S. President – was relabeled Denali.

THE McKINLEY BRIDGE

WHAT A bridge recognizing President William McKinley. No, not him. The other one.

WHERE Between St. Louis and Venice, Ill.

COST None

NOTEWORTHY The McKinley once charged a toll but not these days.

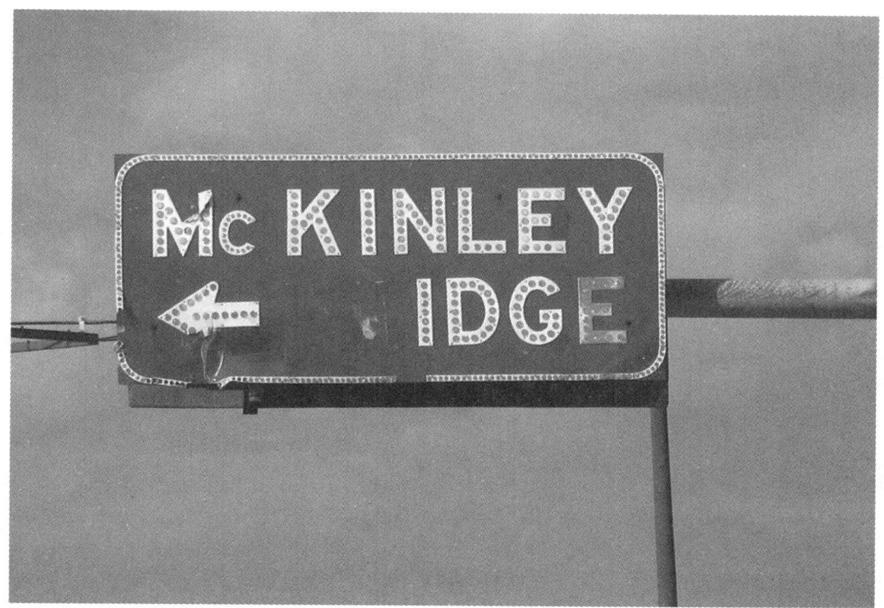

Victorious in the Spanish-American War and known for promotion of energetic American industrial might, President William McKinley was tragically assassinated in 1901. This bridge doesn't honor his accomplishments in any way.

While a bit less regal, the label was plenty appropriate. Opened in 1910 when automobiles were still a rarity, the McKinley was primarily a rail bridge. This explains part of the structure's unusual design, which features lanes on the outside of the trusses. These engineering curiosities were meant to carry vehicles while the center was used by trains. By the mid-20th century, however, the automobile was fast outpacing rail as a preferred mode of transportation, and train traffic eventually disappeared from the bridge.

In fact, by 2001, all traffic was gone from the crumbling span, which had fallen into a shameful state of disrepair. But thanks to local refurbishment efforts, the century-old connector was brought back online in 2007 with cars in the center and pedestrian traffic in the side lanes.

No doubt President McKinley would be proud. Well, one of them would anyway.

72 A PIECE OF 9/11 IN ST. CHARLES COUNTY

Where can you see a part of New York's Twin Towers?

At first glance, the massive 17-foot jumble of twisted, rusting metal in back of the O'Fallon, Missouri, city hall might be dismissed as just another bit of avant garde sculpture. But regrettably, this is no piece of art, and those responsible for its existence weren't pushing the bounds of man's creativity but rather testing his capacity for evil.

This is a chunk of one of New York City's fallen Twin Towers, where nearly 3,000 innocents perished during the biggest terror attack in American history. It was brought to Missouri in 2005 as part of an effort to honor first responders. A nearby plaque immortalizes the names

THE FIRST RESPONDERS' MONUMENT

WHAT: The legacy of terror and the sacrifice of heroes

WHERE: O'Fallon, MO, City Hall, 100 N. Main Street, east parking lot

COST: None

PRO TIP: Inside city hall is a second, much smaller piece of I-beam from the towers covered in flags beneath a transparent case.

A warped piece of steel in St. Charles County serves to recall the horrors of a fateful day when everyone can remember where they were.

of 383 firefighters and police who died during efforts to help civilians in the crippled skyscrapers just before they collapsed.

Difficult as it might be to gaze upon, this piece of history sits as a 22-ton reminder of a day we wish we did not have to remember, recognizing the bravery of those we must never forget.

The first responders' monument was dedicated exactly four years to the day after the attacks in New York, Pennsylvania, and Washington, D.C.

At left, red, white, and blue ribbons wrap the fencing for this tasteful tribute to firefighters, paramedics, and police who protect communities across the nation every day. Below is the small 500-pound hunk of metal resting behind plexiglass within the city hall itself.

73 WHERE A KING SPOKE . . .

Can I visit the site of a Martin Luther King Jr. speech in St. Louis?

You can tell from the start that this isn't just any ordinary library. The arched entryway and domed reading room of this architectural gem don't simply house the research center for the Missouri History Museum. They host a good deal of hidden history themselves.

For starters, this was once a house of worship. Dating to 1927, this imposing structure contained United Hebrew, which was founded in the 1830s and is believed to be the oldest synagogue west of the Mississippi River.

Today, the building is home to roughly 90,000 works ranging from books to magazines and another 60,000 artifacts, all of which tell the story of the region's development.

Whether you want to research the history stored within these walls or simply bask in the significance of the building itself, this library on Skinker is a vital component of the area's rich heritage.

THE MISSOURI HISTORY MUSEUM RESEARCH CENTER

WHAT: St. Louis's most extensive repository of local history

WHERE: 225 S. Skinker Boulevard

COST: Free

PRO TIP: Remember that this is a former synagogue. Be sure to cast your gaze up at the apex of the domed ceiling, where you'll see a Star of David.

In addition, this was also the site of one of Martin Luther King's early addresses in St. Louis. The civil rights leader spoke to more than 2,000 people here in 1960. But this isn't the only place where King gave a speech in town. Other sites graced by the great man's presence include Washington Tabernacle Missionary Baptist Church in the city, Temple Israel in West County, and downtown's Christ Church Cathedral.

United Hebrew's Rabbi Jerome Grollman is said never to have thrown out the chair in his study where King napped before his speech.

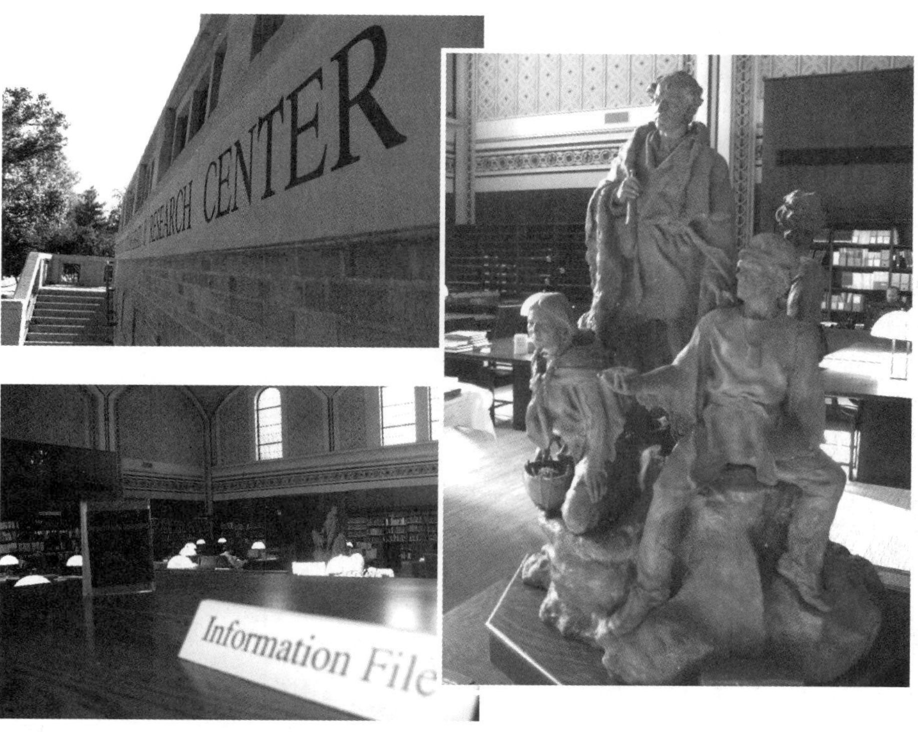

The Missouri History Museum's historical collections were so extensive that it took four months just to move them into the building after the museum acquired the majestic structure at the close of the 1980s. United Hebrew Congregation itself relocated to a new facility in West County, a structure that still houses the synagogue today.

74 SUPREME INJUSTICE

Where is Dred Scott buried?

In a cemetery full of massive, ornately adorned graves, this headstone in the southeast corner of the grounds seems humble enough. A small marker with a simple cross. "Freed from slavery by his friend Taylor Blow," reads the inscription.

Yet, the coins and rocks that top the stone show this is a grave that is honored and loved. The man whose remains lie beneath the sod demanded freedom and raised questions so fundamental about the nature of humanity that it would cost more than half-a-million lives for the nation to answer them.

DRED SCOTT'S GRAVE

WHAT A man who fought the good fight

WHERE Calvary Cemetery, 5239 W. Florissant Avenue

COST None

PRO TIP Headstone hunting can be an interesting and educational activity, but be sure to download the graveyard map before setting out. Calvary's unnamed roads twist wildly and are not laid out in an easy-to-navigate pattern. If you don't know where it is, you won't find it.

Scott passed away in 1858 but wasn't buried here until 1867 after his remains were transferred from a graveyard at Grand and Laclede avenues.

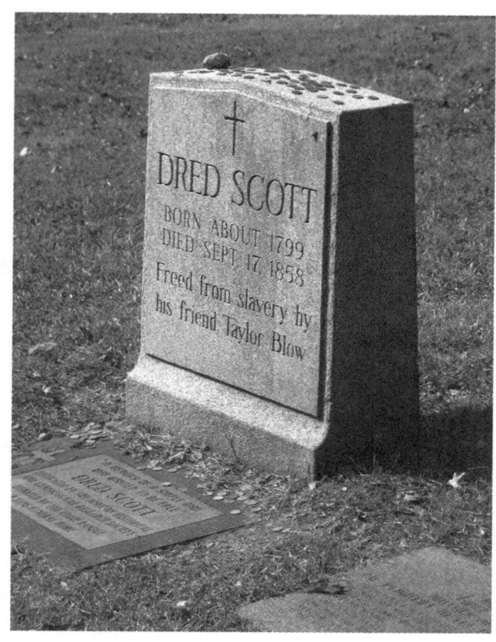

In 1857, a majority of the U.S. Supreme Court found this man was not entitled to basic human rights. History overruled them.

Dred Scott's quest for freedom began in the 1840s when Scott, a slave, petitioned the courts to declare him free since he'd been living in territories where slavery was not allowed. His initial trial in St. Louis was successful; however, appellate courts ruled against him. The case finally reached the United States Supreme Court in 1857, where the court's pro-slavery majority found Scott was not a citizen, but merely property, having, in the infamous words of Chief Justice Roger Taney, "no rights which the white man was bound to respect." The decision returned Scott to servitude and destroyed nearly four decades of political stability caused by the Missouri Compromise by allowing slavery to expand into the territories.

Eventually, the man at the center of the case would become free after being purchased and liberated by a friend shortly before Scott's death.

As for the nation itself, less than three years after Scott died, the deeply divided country was no longer settling such questions in courtrooms but upon battlefields where brother fought brother.

75 THE MAN WHO MADE GEORGIA HOWL

Can I visit the grave of William Tecumseh Sherman?

It is odd that the metro area that contains Grant's Farm isn't also home to the grave of Ulysses S. Grant himself. The old joke "Who is buried in Grant's tomb?" refers to a crypt in New York, not Missouri.

Still, St. Louis is the final resting place for the Union's other famous general, William Tecumseh Sherman, most well-known for his brutal march to the sea. "I can make the march and make Georgia howl!" he said. He did exactly that, leaving Atlanta in ashes in 1864 and presenting Savannah as a Christmas gift to the Union before the year was out.

Sherman's skill as a tactician was unquestioned, although the methods of the general remain controversial to this day. While Sherman was not a cruel man, he was a believer in the idea that combat could not be sugarcoated and believed in pursuing the most direct—if often ruthless—path to victory.

It was an ethos summed up by Sherman's most famous line, "War is hell," a quote for which he is still famous and which—ironically—he probably never uttered, although he did make comments along similar lines in a speech.

General Sherman's middle name came from that of a famous Shawnee chief.

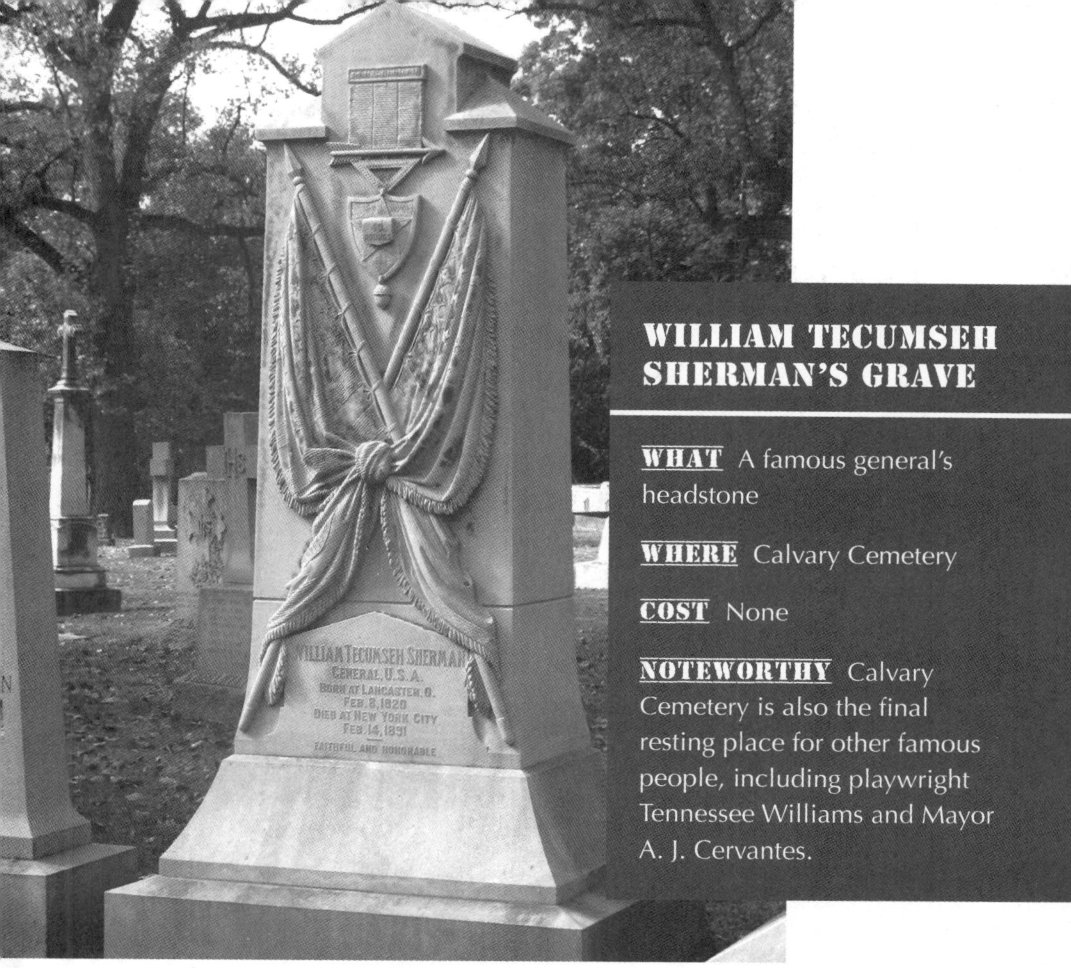

WILLIAM TECUMSEH SHERMAN'S GRAVE

WHAT A famous general's headstone

WHERE Calvary Cemetery

COST None

NOTEWORTHY Calvary Cemetery is also the final resting place for other famous people, including playwright Tennessee Williams and Mayor A. J. Cervantes.

Skilled at the art of war, this general now rests in peace in St. Louis.

Certainly, that philosophy governed his military thinking.

Sometimes, his opponents were also his greatest admirers. Confederate General Joseph E. Johnston, who fought against and ultimately surrendered to Sherman, acted as a pallbearer at his old adversary's funeral. Despite being advised to wear a hat due to the wet February chill, he refused, saying that Sherman would not don headwear if it were Johnston in the coffin.

The thought was prophetic. Perhaps affected by the day's damp weather, Johnston soon fell ill, and he perished of pneumonia shortly thereafter.

76 BREWS AND BIBLES

Where in St. Louis can you have a beer during church services?

Sermons sometimes get a bad reputation as dull, stodgy orations where formality is the rule of the day. While some houses of worship have responded by trying to revamp the church for services, at least one is taking a different approach by moving services out of the church.

That's the idea behind "Bar Church," a program of The Gathering, a United Methodist outfit that began worship in 2006. Bar Church, which meets every Sunday at Humphrey's Restaurant and Tavern across the street from the St. Louis University campus, began in 2014 as a way to engage the local college population. Attendees enjoy good music and a topical message supplemented by camaraderie and toasted ravioli in a fun, casual environment where the communion wine isn't the strongest drink on the menu.

It may look like a standard celebration at your local watering hole, but these are worshippers, not partygoers. And it is the religious message that brings them out to this innovative church service.

THE GATHERING'S BAR CHURCH

WHAT A church service in a pub

WHERE Humphrey's Restaurant and Tavern, 3700 Laclede Avenue

COST Free

PRO TIP Attendees under 21 are welcome at Bar Church, but the minimum drinking age still applies.

But the point, of course, isn't alcohol. It's atmosphere. Organizers say the experiment has been a success and that Bar Church attracts big crowds of mostly younger folks who want to hear relevant spiritual messages that they can apply to their lives while relaxing in a laidback setting.

Humphrey's opened in 1976, although part of the building dates to as early as 1904.

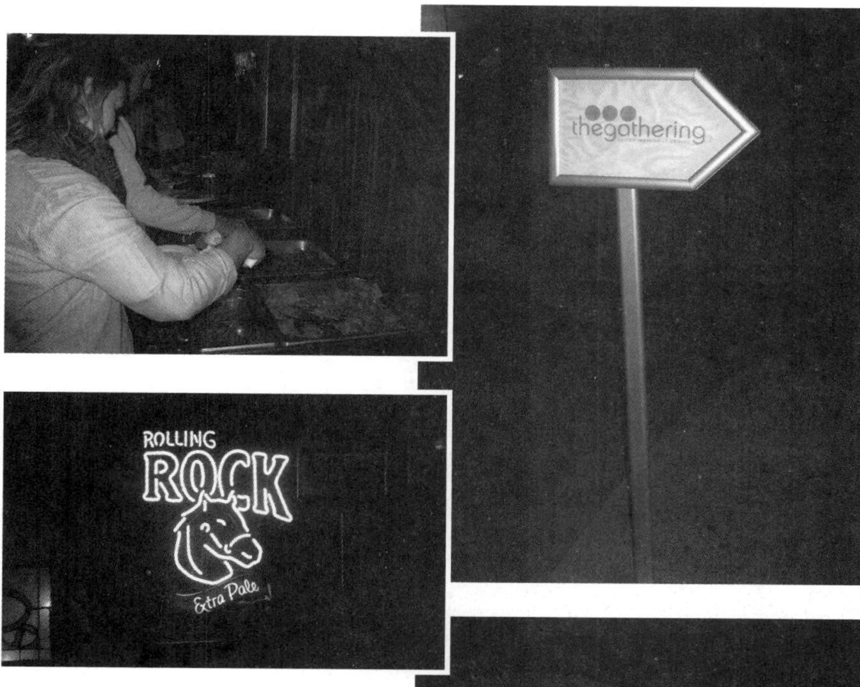

Since 2014, Sunday nights at Humphrey's have included more than good friends and a ballgame on television. The longtime college hangout a stone's throw from St. Louis University now hosts a unique weekly church service sponsored by The Gathering.

77 THE DESIGNS OF YOUTH

What lasting impact did St. Louis have on the design of schools nationwide?

Learning the ABCs has never been as much fun as adults try to make it seem but children of the past undoubtably had more justification to dislike the process than their modern counterparts. Urban schools of the olden days could be remarkably unpleasant places—dim, dreary structures where learning truly felt like a chore.

Enter William B. Ittner. You've probably never heard of Ittner, but if you grew up in the City of St. Louis, you likely spent some time in his creations. As a turn-of-the-century commissioner of school buildings for the Board of Education, Ittner designed dozens of schools across the city and even a

---

MULLANPHY SCHOOL

WHAT The enduring work of an architectural genius who inspired a national movement and made schools more pleasant

WHERE 4221 Shaw Avenue

COST Free

NOTEWORTHY Ittner's ability with schools didn't stop him from designing other edifices in the area, including the Scottish Rite Cathedral, the Missouri Athletic Club, and the Continental Life Building.

An architectural firm in the St. Louis area still bears the Ittner family name.

Mullanphy School on the Southside was Ittner's final St. Louis school design.

few in the county. Most of them still stand today and some are on the National Register of Historic Places. His work includes such prominent names as Lafayette, Blow, and Sumner. The *Distilled History* blog notes that Soldan High School was particularly noted for its beauty, with lavatories and locker rooms "being compared to fine hotels of the day."

But the architect's influence goes far beyond the St. Louis area. His designs incorporating windows, natural lighting, and indoor plumbing became a model for the nation and led to his laying out more than 400 buildings coast-to-coast. Architects and educators flocked to St. Louis just to learn his methods, with half of American states having at least one Ittner school.

As of 2012, four dozen Ittner schools remained in the area. Built between 1898 and 1915, they display his signature style, which made the classroom a bit less horrible a place for a young person to spend a sunny day. Stop by his last masterpiece, Mullanphy School on Shaw Avenue, to check out his work for yourself.

78 KEYS TO THE CITY

Why does this Metro station have a huge set of car keys out front?

In any city, public transit can be a somewhat dull, functional affair. That's one of the reasons that transit authorities often try to spice up the ride a bit by dropping in items of artistic interest along the way. Sometimes that can have an element of whimsy to it.

That's the reason that riders of Metro trains through Pagedale can have the experience of seeing what appears to be the contents of a giant's pockets emptied out onto a set of stairs.

Honey, Where's My Metro Pass? has graced the Rock Road station along Metro's Red Line since 2010, when its

---

As of 2013, Metro was logging 17 million boardings annually.

HONEY, WHERE'S MY METRO PASS?

WHAT Public art

WHERE Rock Road Metro station

COST Free unless you ride the train

NOTEWORTHY Metro's millionth rider boarded the system just over a month after it opened in 1993.

It may just be a work of art, but the truth is that it'd be pretty hard to lose this set of car keys.

metal and fiberglass elements, including spare change, lip balm, and a crumpled slip of paper marked "receipt," were laid in place under the watchful eyes of SIUE art faculty Nick Lang and Thad Duhigg. Interns from St. Louis ArtWorks also contributed to the effort, which their ideas helped to inspire.

79 IN THE BUFF . . .

Where can you go to find a nudist resort in the area?

All Missourians may be in the Show Me State, but some take the idea more literally than others. At the Forty Acre Club in Franklin County, you can indeed experience the concept of life without clothes at the area's premiere nudist resort.

Despite its name, the Forty Acre Club now owns an area twice that size. Founded in 1951, the resort has both full- and part-time residents and also accepts guests for a limited number of spots during non-winter months. Designed for couples and families, the club is a member of the American Association for Nude Recreation and holds regular activities ranging from trivia parties to water volleyball. Special events might include dances, potlucks, or perhaps a chili cook-off. The calendar for 2014 even listed a "Nude Year Party" for late December.

THE FORTY ACRE CLUB

WHAT Nudism in St. Louis

WHERE 104 Ridge Acres Loop, Lonedell, Mo.

COST $304-$612 annually for membership depending on level and type. Rental units range from $27-$32 most of the time.

PRO TIP Devices with cameras are prohibited on the grounds. Also, for sanitary reasons, you should expect to always sit on a towel.

Some club members who own property at the resort have been there for more than 50 years.

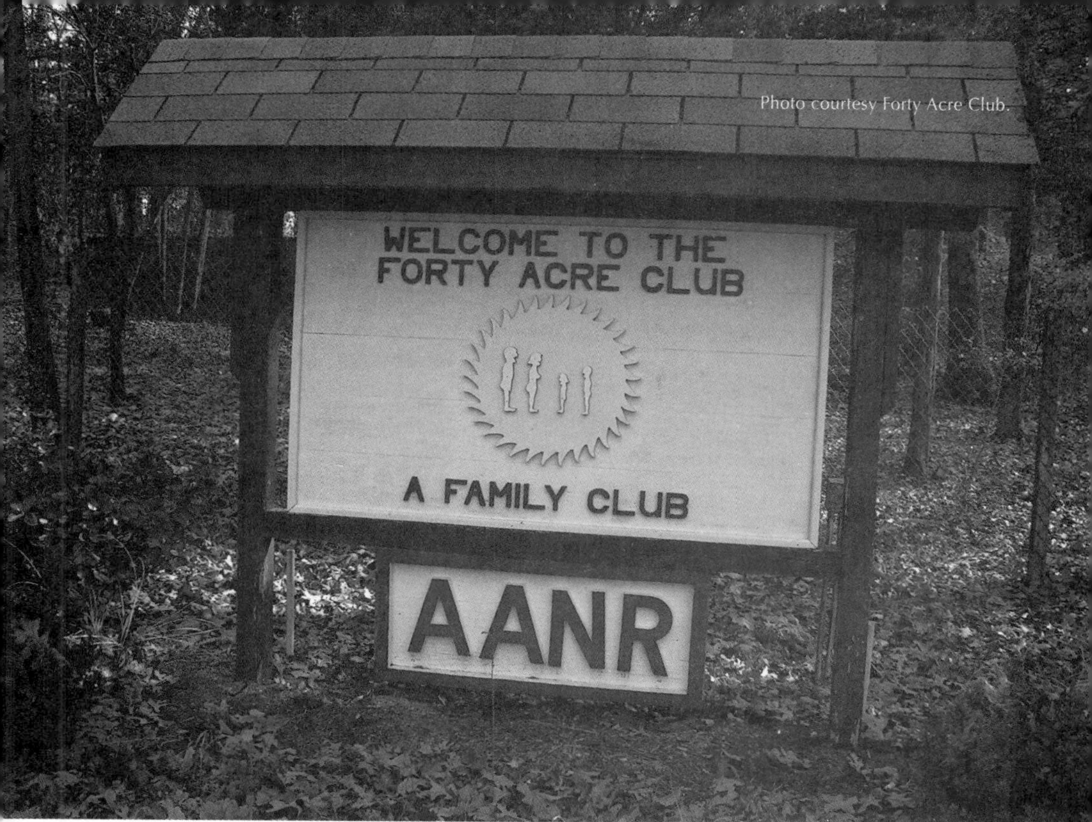

The nudist ethos is alive and well in Franklin County, where the Forty Acre Club has been in existence for more than 60 years.

Spa services on-site include therapeutic massage, and members can take advantage of the forested hiking trails and undeveloped wilderness the club has to offer. RV spaces are also available.

Please note that nudism is not exhibitionism. It is not about sex and is not a show for gawkers to "get an eyeful." These are nice people. If you don't have a genuine interest in the lifestyle, don't show up and pester those who do. There are also strict policies in place to prevent anti-social or inappropriate behavior. Moreover, if you are there, you are expected to be unclothed. Single male guests are accepted only by reservation. Call ahead or consult the website at www.fortyacreclub.com for full policies and details.

80 THE REAL ROOTS OF GOVERNMENT

Where was the first Missouri governor sworn in?

Most area residents learned in Missouri history class that the first state capital was in St. Charles. True enough.

But if you want to be technical about it, the state's government was really born in St. Louis—right there amidst the bars and restaurants of today's Laclede's Landing, in fact. The first state legislative session took place here at the site of what was then the Missouri Hotel in the autumn of 1820. Alexander McNair, Missouri's initial chief executive, was also inaugurated on the spot, and its U.S. senators were chosen on-site as well. A historical plaque commemorates these events, which—for better or worse—represent the true beginnings of state government in Missouri.

Thomas Hart Benton, one of the first two senators selected at the Missouri Hotel, is now in the National Statuary Hall in Washington, D.C.

THE MISSOURI HOTEL

WHAT Where state government began

WHERE 727 N. First Street

COST Due every April 15

NOTEWORTHY The capital moved to Jefferson City in 1826.

ON THIS SITE STOOD THE OLD MISSOURI HOTEL. THE FIRST LEGISLATURE CONVENED HERE UNDER THE FIRST STATE CONSTITUTION ON SEPTEMBER 18, 1820, THE YEAR BEFORE MISSOURI WAS ADMITTED TO THE UNION. IT WAS ALSO THE SITE OF THE INAUGURATION OF THE FIRST GOVERNOR OF MISSOURI, ALEXANDER McNAIR AND OF THE ELECTION OF THE STATE'S FIRST U.S. SENATORS DAVID BARTON AND THOMAS HART BENTON.
FREDERIC RAEDER DESIGNED THE CURRENT BUILDING FOR THE CHRISTIAN PEPER TOBACCO COMPANY IN 1874. THE SAME YEAR THE EADS BRIDGE WAS COMPLETED. IT IS ONE OF THE LARGEST CAST IRON FRONT BUILDINGS IN THIS COUNTRY. RAEDER PLACE IS LISTED AS ONE OF THE 500 SIGNIFICANT ARCHITECTURAL STRUCTURES IN THE U.S.
IN 1976 THE ARCHITECTURAL FIRM OF KIMBLE A. COHN ASSOCIATES REMODELED THE BUILDING FOR OFFICES AND RESTAURANTS AS PART OF THE REDEVELOPMENT OF LACLEDE'S LANDING. THE RAEDER PLACE BUILDING IS VIRTUALLY INTACT FROM THE TIME OF ITS CONSTRUCTION.

Despite St. Charles' claims to the title, the first defacto seat of political power was in St. Louis just north of the Arch.

The Missouri Hotel, of course, has long since stopped accepting guests. The building that replaced it was built after the Civil War to house a tobacco operation. Now known as Raeder Place, it was revamped in 1976.

So next time you motor down First Capitol Drive in St. Charles, you'll know the true story. State political power was birthed on the banks of the Mississippi, not the Missouri.

81 CAREER LIFTOFF

Where can you take a Harvard-level computer programming course for free?

Bobbing in the twin wakes of the information revolution and the global economic crisis, we live in an increasingly fluid world where vocational paths are far twistier than they once were. New jobs in exciting fields are available, but how can you afford the cost of retraining to become a high-powered computer programmer?

Yet what if that cost were zero?

In St. Louis, it is.

That's thanks to LaunchCode, a remarkable nonprofit initiative that has helped train and place dozens of individuals in computer-related fields. The idea behind the program, which blasted off in 2013, was to offer a pathway for those who have an interest in the burgeoning world of technology but who don't have formal job experience

---

LAUNCHCODE MENTOR CENTER

WHAT A way to launch into the world of computer programming

WHERE 4811 Delmar Boulevard

COST Amazingly, it is free

NOTEWORTHY In addition to its other initiatives, LaunchCode also runs CoderGirl, an all-female meetup for programmers.

As of early 2015, LaunchCode had placed at least 130 St. Louisans in apprenticeships.

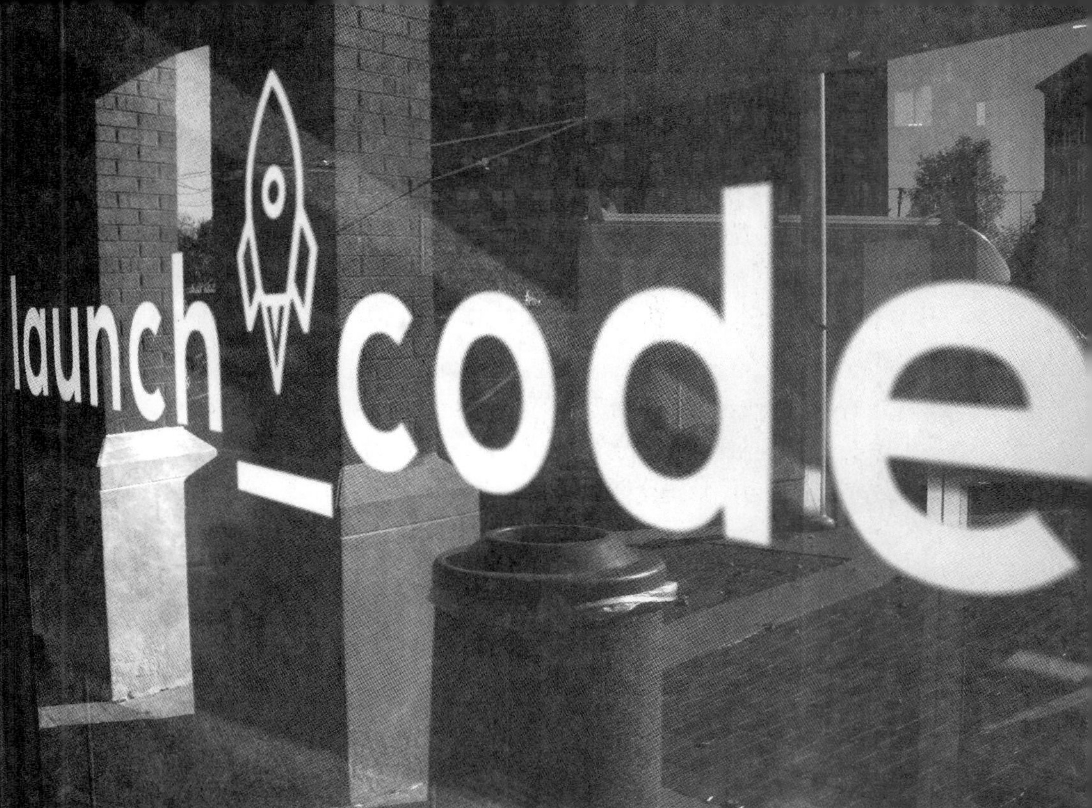

Though it started two years earlier, LaunchCode didn't open its mentor center on Delmar until 2015. Now it has a physical location to help area residents get in on the St. Louis tech boom.

or a college degree. According to government analysts, the growing gap created by such barriers could leave as many a million programming jobs unfilled by 2020, while countless people remain in low-wage positions because they lack traditional credentials. LaunchCode provides both a two-week beginner course and access to classes in conjunction with a Harvard-level online offering known as CS50. For those who demonstrate ability, apprenticeships and contacts with major companies are available.

The enterprise, in part the brainchild of local entrepreneur Jim McKelvey, has become so promising that it is beginning to expand nationally. It was even cited as a model by President Barack Obama during his rollout of the federal TechHire program.

82 THE INDIAN OF JEFFERSON AVENUE

Why does even the creator of this Southside landmark dislike it?

Art is the sort of field where one man's trash is another's treasure. Sometimes, it can be so esoteric that only the artist himself can truly appreciate his own work.

Then again, sometimes you can't even count on that.

Such is the case with the 13-foot tall, stony-faced Native American who has spent the last three decades welcoming visitors to the corner of South Jefferson Boulevard and Cherokee Street.

The work, commissioned by local business owners, was created by Bill Christman, who was decidedly ambivalent about his role in the well-known landmark, saying that its proportions didn't come out satisfactorily. When asked by a local journalist in 2007 if he wished to take credit for the fiberglass-coated icon, he replied, "To my everlasting mortification, I was the sculptor of that."

Strangely, there isn't even general agreement on when the statue went up. According to the article, one media account indicates late 1985, but the sculptor, misidentified in that account as "Bill Christmas," said it was earlier.

Despite its imposing size, the statue itself has a lightweight core of foam and only clocks in at about 200 pounds.

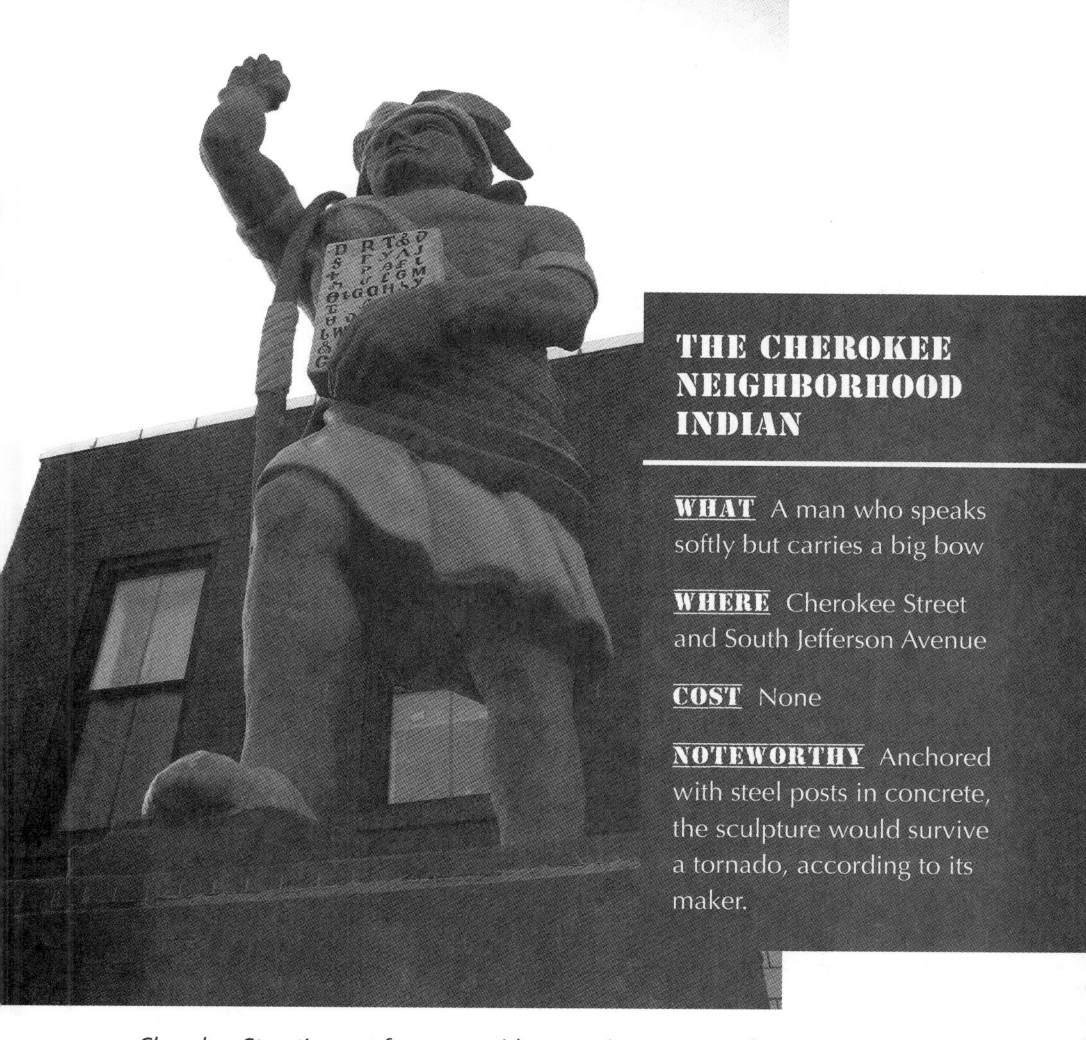

THE CHEROKEE NEIGHBORHOOD INDIAN

WHAT A man who speaks softly but carries a big bow

WHERE Cherokee Street and South Jefferson Avenue

COST None

NOTEWORTHY Anchored with steel posts in concrete, the sculpture would survive a tornado, according to its maker.

Cherokee Street's most famous resident continues to stand watch over the busy intersection at South Jefferson.

Others in the area are a bit more generous toward the landmark. Some see the grimacing chief as a unique figure in the area, representing the quirky, gritty, and somewhat offbeat nature of the Cherokee neighborhood.

Regardless, the big fellow seems to be here to stay.

83 CHAIN REACTION

Where can you be a "hacker" in St. Louis?

In today's world, hackers get a bad rap. Mention the term and everyone immediately wants to change their computer password. But the fact is that "hackerspaces" like Arch Reactor here in St. Louis are flourishing with a much different kind of hacker who has nothing to do with cyber mischief. Part of the "maker movement," these "hackers" are simply creative DIY specialists who love to build things. From woodworking to computer geekery to the emerging art of 3D printing, hackerspaces give both a place to work and a sense of community to folks who enjoy engaging their hands and their minds on engineering challenges.

Originally working out of a gritty building on South Jefferson, the busy workshop littered with boxes, castoff equipment, old toys, and tools ranging from a micro lathe to a laser cutter is set to move to a new home on Scott Avenue as of early 2016. Members have built everything from camera-equipped balloons designed to reach space to a

ARCH REACTOR

WHAT A hackerspace for the maker in you

WHERE 2215 Scott Avenue

COST Memberships range from free to $45 depending on the level

PRO TIP Arch Reactor holds special "Hack Something" events on Sunday nights. Check archreactor.org for details.

One of only a handful of hackerspaces in Missouri, Arch Reactor, founded in 2009, can give you the tools and the talent to release your inner maker.

carbon dioxide-powered sandwich gun for shooting hoagies across the room to an internet-connected cookie jar that warns loved ones when you try to cheat on your diet. Others construct their own circuit boards or even do comparatively down-to-earth activities like sewing and crafts projects.

This unique nonprofit sprang to life in 2009 in a conversation between friends over pizza and today has dozens of members and hosts all manner of special events.

Full membership at Arch Reactor with 24/7 access to the space requires that the applicant be voted in by members.

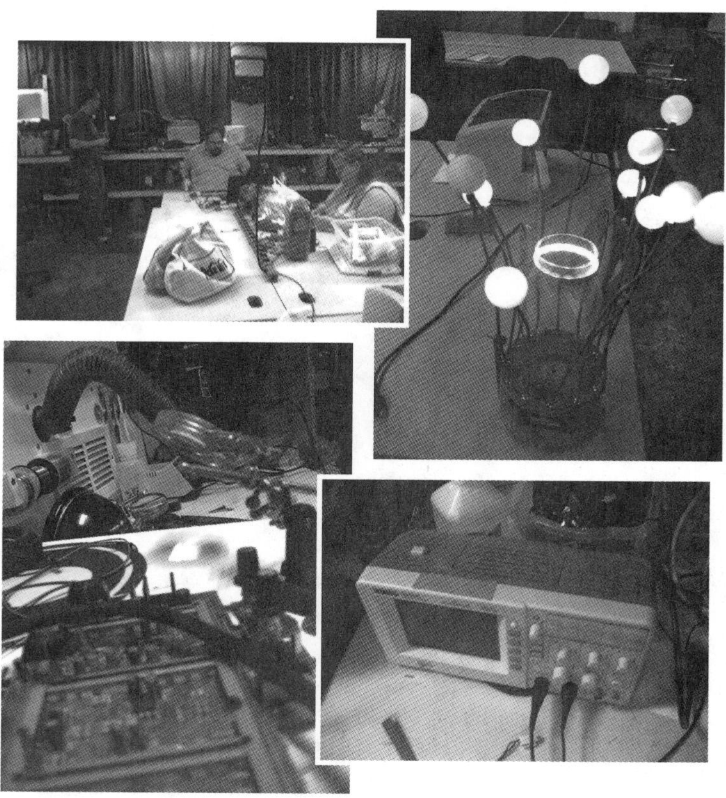

For the amateur tinkerer in all of us, the items strewn about the workshop floor at Arch Reactor are a gold mine of new ideas and skills to augment and explore.

84 "ROME OF THE WEST"

Where can you see one of the largest mosaic collections in the Western Hemisphere?

Sometimes called the "Rome of the West" by its admirers, St. Louis has a noteworthy Catholic history, and nowhere can it be better understood than beneath the majestic domes of the Cathedral Basilica of St. Louis.

Named as a basilica in 1997 by Pope John Paul II, this breathtaking building is as stunning in its scope as it is superior in its beauty. Quiet candles of remembrance glow in nearby alcoves as awed visitors stroll beneath a dizzying 143-foot high central skylight flanked by mosaics of the Holy Trinity, the Prophet Ezekiel, and other religious figures, while 16 angels float above arrays of stars.

The Cathedral Basilica of St. Louis is astounding for those of any faith to behold.

CATHEDRAL BASILICA OF ST. LOUIS

WHAT The story of creation in the medium of tile

WHERE 4431 Lindell Boulevard

COST Free, however, there is a $2 charge for entrance to the Mosaic Museum downstairs

PRO TIP This facility has plenty to see, and visitors are welcome to wander its corridors until 5 p.m., but remember it is also a place of active worship. Avoid touring or gawking during the daily masses, which take place twice in the morning and once at midday. Guided tours will also require a reservation.

Despite hefty arrangements of statuary and the lovely stained glass, it is the tile work that makes this facility special. The basilica contains one of the most impressive collections of mosaics in the world, comprising more than 80,000 square feet and a mind-boggling 41.5 million individual pieces. Work continued for more than three-quarters of a century before completion in 1988. A special museum has even been set up in the basement level of the structure to explore the beauty, the craft, and the science of mosaics.

Construction got underway on the Cathedral Basilica in 1907 under Cardinal John Glennon.

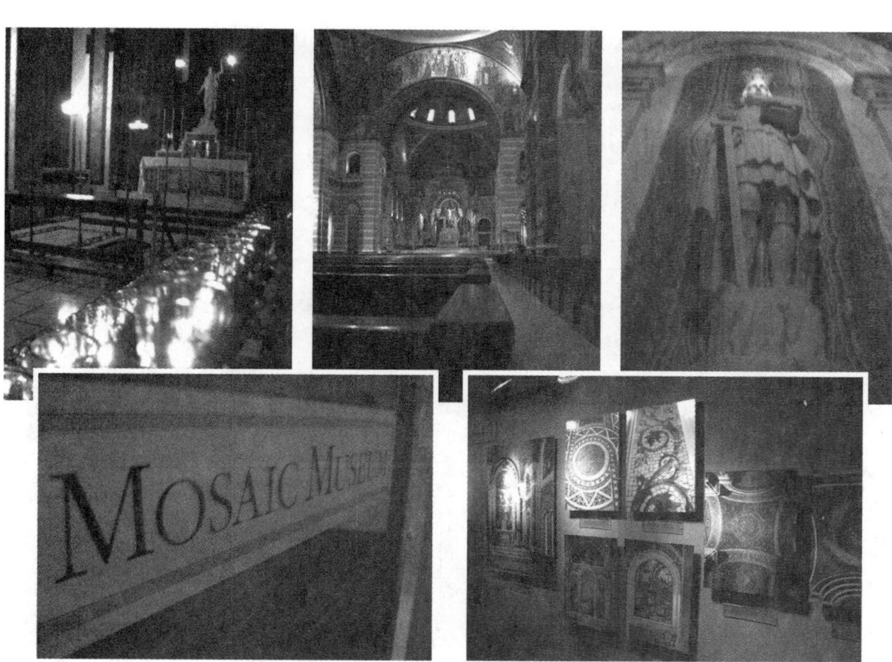

The Mosaic Museum is only one of the many highlights of this Midwestern gem of spiritual enlightenment. You can also check out the statuary collection, which includes a representation of St. Louis himself.

85 A RAIL WORKER'S DELIGHT

Does this municipality really owe its name to a lazy railroad worker?

Town names can sometimes be head-scratchers. Some, like Truth-or-Consequences, New Mexico, might be named after a game show, while others, like North Pole, Alaska, have turned their moniker into a tourist attraction.

One might think that Eureka, in western St. Louis County, got its name from the more famous California Gold Rush city with that title, but in fact, that's not the case. Missouri's Eureka, which means "I've found it" in ancient Greek, allegedly received its moniker due to the railroad. According to the town website, an 1850s rail worker was laying track out of the bluffs outside of town and was

---

The nearby settlement of Pacific straddling the Franklin County border is also supposed to owe its name to the railroad, the Missouri-Pacific.

EUREKA

WHAT A cry of relief immortalized for the ages

WHERE I-44 west of the Meramec River

COST None

NOTEWORTHY Six Flags has been Eureka's biggest tourist draw since 1970.

Though it has been inhabited since before the Civil War, the Interstate 44 town of Eureka wasn't incorporated officially until 1954, roughly a century after its beginnings.

thrilled to finally see a stretch of straight, flat land upon which to work. He supposedly shouted "Eureka!" and his cry of joy remains a part of the suburb's history to this day.

While the name's origin sounds a bit dubious, it is indeed possible, and I can't think of a better explanation. Either way, it is part of the town's official history, and it makes a nice story to think that an entire municipality may owe its identity to a poor fellow tired of dragging rails and ties through the hills.

86 METALLIC MYSTERY

Why do upright panels of rusting metal take up an entire block of downtown?

Some take quizzical note of it. Many just try to ignore it. But for most, the massive, vaguely triangular arrangement of rusting steel plates that stands defiantly north of busy Market Street seems an odd enigma. Numbering eight, the weathered 40-foot slabs of metal sit in an otherwise barren acre of parched grass on a presumably valuable tract nestled between 10th and 11th streets, abutted by the majestic city courts building on one side and the attractively trendy Citygarden venue on the other. What is this strange object? A secret government project? A failed construction effort? A cautionary testament to the dangers of oxidation?

In fact, this piece of public art is a brainchild of Richard Serra, the creative mind whose works in sheet metal are famous the world over. Officially, this block is a sculpture

---

Serra's 2000 sculpture *Joe* is a tribute to Joseph Pulitzer Jr., who commissioned an early major outdoor work from the artist.

TWAIN

WHAT A sculpture of heavily rusted metal

WHERE The city block bordered by 10th, 11th, Market, and Chestnut streets

COST Free except for the parking meter

NOTEWORTHY *Twain* is not a true triangle. One of the eight panels is 10 feet longer than the others.

Now in its fourth decade, the vaguely inexplicable Serra sculpture Twain continues to loom strangely between Market and Chestnut Streets as one of the more unique art projects in the area.

park bearing Serra's name, although this is the only sculpture in it. The avant garde work, titled *Twain*, was controversial from its start. Many simply didn't understand its purpose, and proposals for the piece were held up for several years—in part due to public uncertainty over the design—before federal funding finally pushed the idea off the drawing boards in 1981. Since then, *Twain*, which was supposed to provide a walled haven from city bustle for urban dwellers, has remained an object of curiosity—and occasional derision—as well as a home to everything from pickup wiffleball games to the work of the city's graffiti practitioners.

Unfortunately, art doesn't always come out as intended. A third of the trees planned for the site perished. Upkeep by the city has been lackluster at times. The benches and lampposts slated for installation never happened at all. Yet, *Twain* remains.

87 EXPERIENCING THE STILL LIFE

Where can you have a sleepover at a wax museum?

Admit it. There are times you want to see Batman, an imperial storm trooper, and a St. Louis Cardinal all in one spot.

Welcome to 720 North Second Street, home of St. Louis's very own Laclede's Landing Wax Museum. Boasting "the most photographed lobby in St. Louis," the institution has more than 200 figures spread across 10,000 square feet. Movie stars mingle with sports icons, world leaders, and fictional characters. The quirky institution even has a "chamber of horrors" and "torture animatronics" for those who aren't too faint of heart.

Founded in 1983, the wax museum is housed in a historic late-19th-century building.

LACLEDE'S LANDING WAX MUSEUM

WHAT A chance to wax nostalgic

WHERE 720 North Second Street

COST $3-$10 depending on age

PRO TIP Hours vary so call ahead before making the trip.

Divided among five levels, the Laclede's Landing Wax Museum is a true St. Louis original covering everything from superheroes to alien beings. Also, don't forget to try their legendary ice cream.

And, yes, indeed, for the right price, you and as many as 149 of your closest friends can do an overnight lock-in at the wax museum. There's plenty of food and drink on hand and off-duty cops provide security. You'll be let out at 8 a.m.

If you would prefer to have the fun come to your home instead, the museum actually rents out figures. The cost for your waxy guest starts at $300.

88 AN UNPLEASANT AWAKENING

Why is a giant escaping from the earth in Chesterfield?

When you get right down to it, no one likes to get up in the morning. Still, one can imagine that the process is even less pleasant if you've discovered yourself buried alive. That's the concept behind *The Awakening,* a remarkable, five-piece aluminum masterwork from the fertile mind of J. Seward Johnson that is situated at present in the confines of a Chesterfield park.

Weighing more than two tons, the sculpture features a less-than-happy 70-foot-tall giant attempting to burst from the earth after what must have been a very sound sleep. Parts of all four limbs erupt out of the Central Park grass, with the big fellow's right arm clawing skyward to a height of about 17 feet.

Erected in 2009, this is one of two *Awakenings* in the nation. Its sister statue has been attempting to wrench itself from the soil of a Maryland waterfront just outside Washington, D.C., since 1980.

At its installation, the sculpture was estimated to have a net worth of almost $1 million.

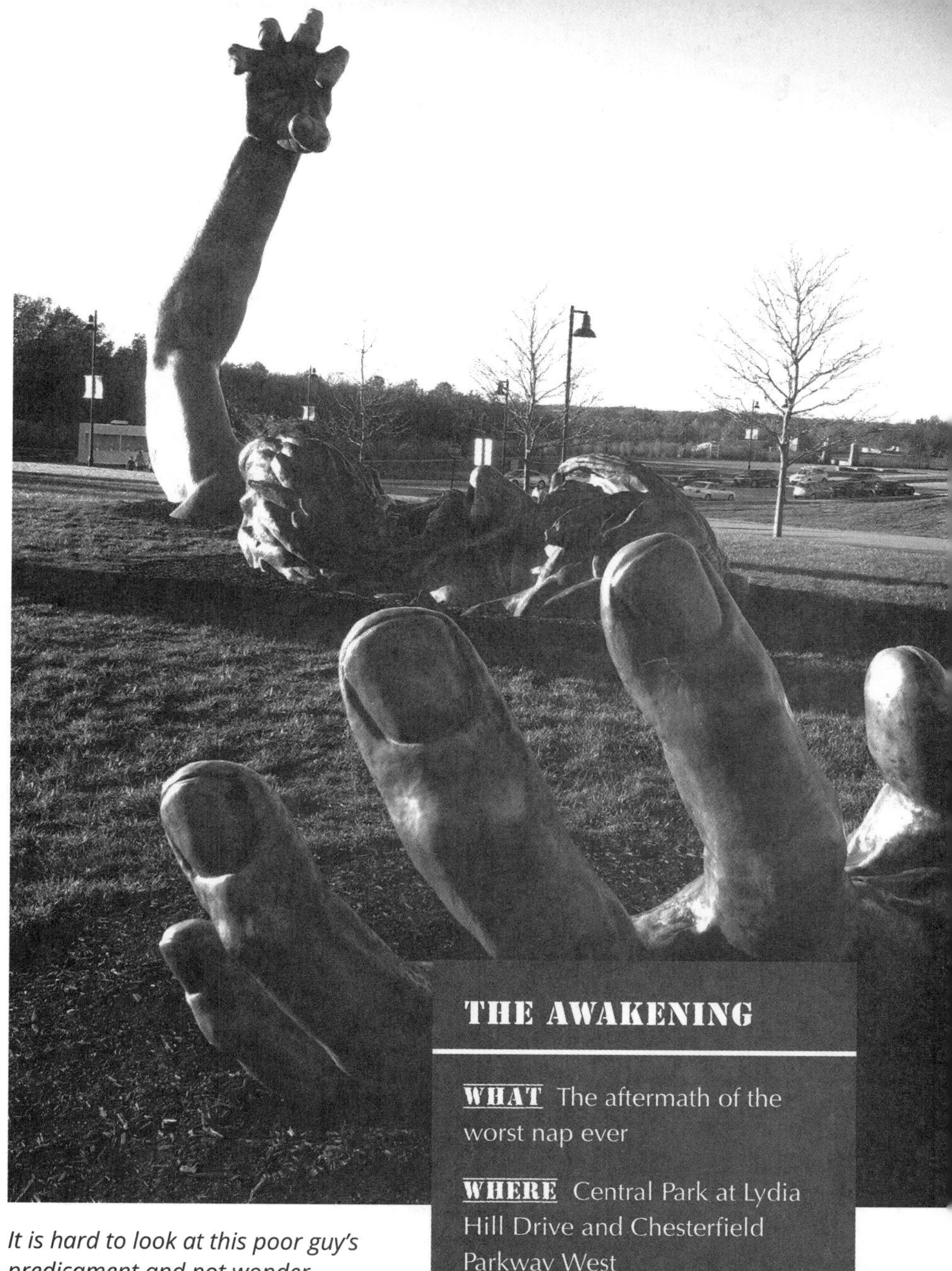

It is hard to look at this poor guy's predicament and not wonder what exactly he must have been doing the night before.

THE AWAKENING

WHAT The aftermath of the worst nap ever

WHERE Central Park at Lydia Hill Drive and Chesterfield Parkway West

COST None

PRO TIP Bring the kids. Playing on the giant is a favorite activity of the younger set.

89 MIRACLE ON 11TH STREET

Where is the site of the only officially recognized miracle in the Midwest?

Applied to everything from baseball playoff victories to cleaning products to sandwich toppings, the word "miracle" has been robbed by the modern world of much of its original sense of divine awe.

And yet, the Catholic Church does still have an official process for recognizing events it finds to be beyond natural explanation. Just such an event happened in St. Louis during the 1860s when a laborer named Ignatius Strecker took severely ill due to infection after an injury. Diagnosed as a hopeless case, the desperate man kissed a relic of Peter Claver, a 17th-century Spanish Jesuit priest. Previously thought to be at death's door, Strecker suddenly began to recover, even showing up to work the following morning. Within two weeks, the man's ailments were but a memory and he went on to live until 1880, cured of tuberculosis by the relic of a man whose name he didn't even previously know.

Today, the shrine where Strecker's road to wellness began remains a beloved landmark on 11th Street, and mass is still held here on Sundays at 11 a.m. sharp. Tours of the facility, which was built in 1846, are available directly afterward.

The shrine's Altar of Answered Prayers was built by parishioners who believed that St. Joseph spared them from an 1866 cholera outbreak.

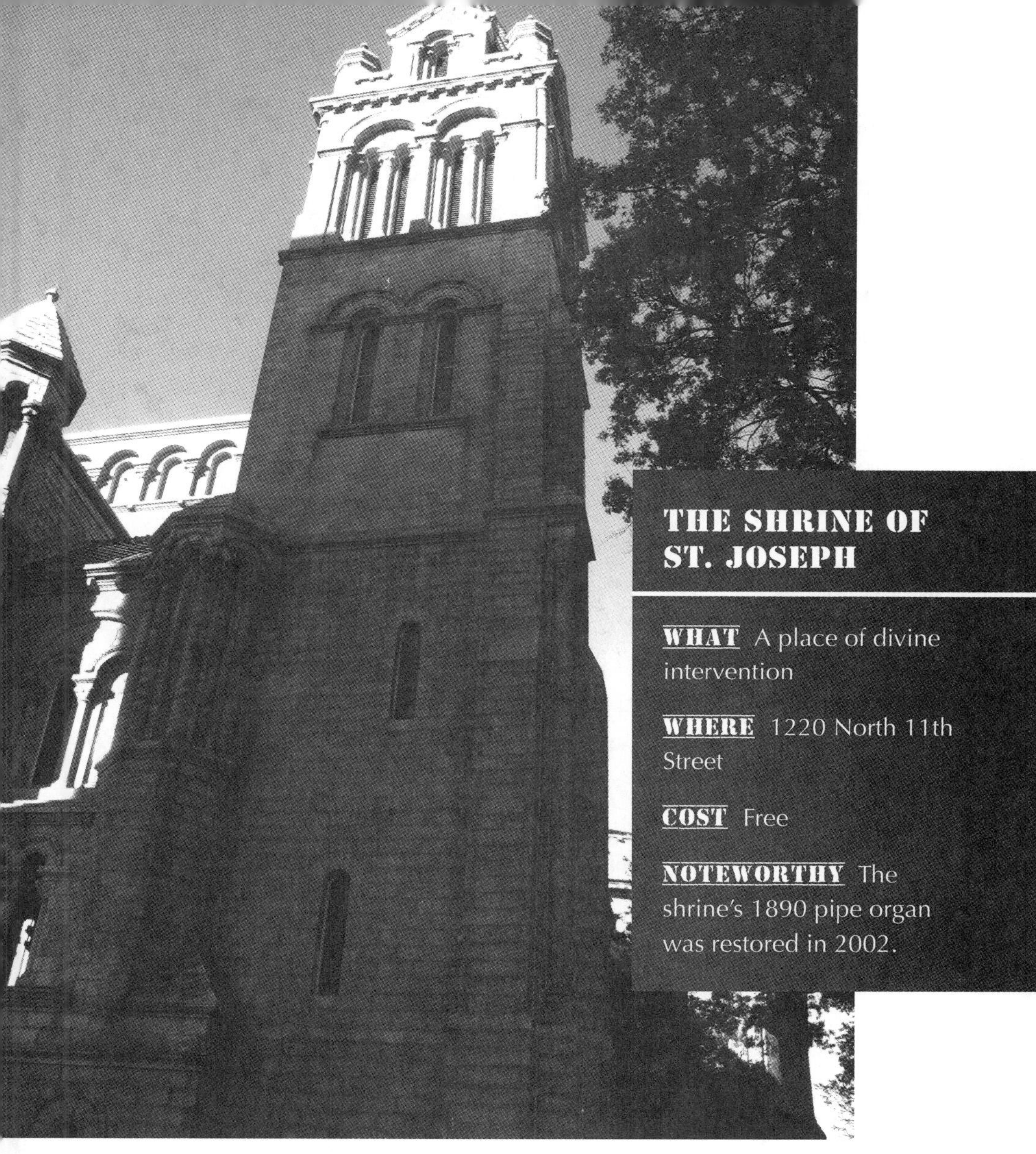

THE SHRINE OF ST. JOSEPH

WHAT A place of divine intervention

WHERE 1220 North 11th Street

COST Free

NOTEWORTHY The shrine's 1890 pipe organ was restored in 2002.

Even without the Miracle of Peter Claver, the Shrine of St. Joseph would rank among the region's most historic churches.

The case of Ignatius Strecker continues to inspire people of faith to this day, and seven years after the man's death, Claver was made a saint, thanks in part to the only officially recognized miracle ever to take place in the Midwest—and it happened right here in St. Louis.

90 ST. ANN'S QUEEN OF THE DRIVE-IN

Why is a local grocery store promoted by a giant baton twirler?

To younger North Countians, the smiling visage of the neon-fringed majorette who greets shoppers as they swing into St. Ann's Airway Centre for milk and bread at the local grocery may seem just another piece of gaudy Americana meant to catch the eye of potential customers from the main road.

But in reality the sweet-faced redhead who towers above the intersection of St. Charles Rock Road and St. Timothy has a history that goes back far longer than the recently built shopping center she now promotes. She's one of the few vestiges of the nostalgic drive-in era still standing in the region.

Of course her days of hawking films are over. Dating to just after WWII, the ever-grinning maiden now welcomes patrons to the local Shop 'n Save with a merry kicking leg and spinning baton, just as she did for more than three decades of visitors to the Airway Drive-In until its closure during the 1980s. The neon on her snappy blue and gold uniform is still lit each night, though these days the panels beneath her fashionable boots advertise the prices for regular unleaded and diesel at the nearby gas pumps rather than double features from Hollywood's dream machine.

The last remaining operational drive-in theater in the area is the Skyview in Belleville, Illinois.

THE MASSIVE MAJORETTE

WHAT One of the last beautiful reminders that St. Louis once had a thriving drive-in culture

WHERE 10634 St. Charles Rock Road

COST Free, unless you are buying groceries or gas, of course

PRO TIP Visit at night. Neon art lacks much of its pizzazz when the sun is out.

This huge neon lady never seems to show her age. She is not just a treasured landmark but a relic of a bygone era of moviedom.

91 BEING A BIT VELODROMATIC

Who on earth is Mr. BumpyFace? What is a velodrome and why should we feel honored to have one in St. Louis?

Admit it. You probably haven't met Mr. BumpyFace. You probably also have no idea what a velodrome is. Still, you can take a bit of hometown pride in knowing that St. Louis doesn't just have a velodrome, but has one of only 27 such facilities in the entire country. A special kind of cycling arena, our Penrose Park Velodrome has been around since 1962, having replaced its predecessor in Forest Park. It still holds races each Thursday night.

The velodrome was a one-time host of the U.S. National Track Cycling Championships.

PENROSE PARK VELODROME

WHAT An excellent cycling venue

WHERE Penrose Park (I-70 and Kingshighway)

COST $10 to race

PRO TIP There is no lot. Parking is on the grass.

Last resurfaced just a decade ago, "Mr. BumpyFace" still brings smiles to competitive cyclists across the area during its regular Thursday night events.

But a half-century of wear and tear can take a toll on anyone. Hence the affectionate nickname for the banked biking track whose asphalt surface has sustained more than a few bumps, dips, and waves over the years. Have fun trying out, but remember, these aren't the bikes you are used to. Velodrome cycles are fixed-gear, single-speed devices.

Oh, yes, and did I mention they don't have brakes? Happy riding.

92 HAZELWOOD TO THE HIGH COURT

What famous Supreme Court case started in North County?

When the principal at Hazelwood East High School saw articles in the *Spectrum* student newspaper tackling topics like divorce and teen pregnancy, he found himself so deeply concerned over privacy issues for the subjects of the pieces that he removed the articles from the issue altogether. Cathy Kuhlmeier and two others on staff disagreed. The pages were dropped, but it was a dispute that would go on well past deadline.

The resulting legal fight would drag on for more than four years before it finally reached the United States Supreme Court in Hazelwood School District v. Kuhlmeier, a landmark 1988 case in which the justices ultimately ruled

Until a 2003 renovation, Hazelwood East was an "open classroom" school where rooms were not closed off from one another.

HAZELWOOD EAST HIGH SCHOOL

WHAT The bounds of journalistic freedom

WHERE 11300 Dunn Road

COST None

NOTEWORTHY The plaintiffs based much of their claim on an earlier matter in which students were allowed to wear armbands to protest the Vietnam War.

First opened in 1974, Hazelwood East High School was the setting for one of the modern era's most notable press freedom cases.

that the district's actions were reasonable. The students, who had prevailed at the appellate level, had their victory reversed by the 5-3 decision, which continues to be a controlling precedent in case law to this day.

While the court found that a school could not remove its students' First Amendment rights to free expression of personal beliefs, it also found that the district had a right to maintain its "basic educational mission" and that the constitutional freedoms of students operating within school walls were not automatically the same as those of adults in the outside world.

Kuhlmeier was a major ruling that helped define the rights—and the limits—of student media—and it began right off of Interstate 270.

93 RECORDING HEROISM

Where can you see Stan Musial's or Jack Buck's military records?

Archival work is hardly the most glamorous of occupations. Yet beyond the rows of musty books and manila folders, there is real heroism to be recorded, and thanks to the National Personnel Records Center, St. Louis is home to the largest collection of American military records in the country save for Washington, D.C., itself.

An estimated 9 billion pages' worth of material resides at this North County facility comprising roughly 100 million files, including more than 56 million military records dating back as early as 1841. The trove of information, both military and civilian, is so massive that it took 49 semitrailer trucks five days just to move it all when the building opened in 2011.

But the facility isn't just a "fill it and forget it" storehouse. The center receives as many as 5,000 requests daily with an astounding 90 percent of the National Archives and Records Administration's reference activity occurring right here in St. Louis for records in the center's quarter-million square feet of storage space.

NATIONAL PERSONNEL RECORDS CENTER

WHAT A massive cache of information

WHERE 1 Archives Drive off Dunn Road

COST Varies based on the record you seek

PRO TIP Phone ahead at 314-801-0850 to schedule an appointment if you wish to use the research room.

Costing $115 million dollars to construct, this North County records facility houses so many records that if its file boxes were laid end-to-end, they would reach all the way to Dallas, Texas.

Some of those requests are from veterans looking to prove their service and establish their eligibility for certain benefits. That's been a difficult task due to a fire at the previous records facility that destroyed about 18 million files. Using advanced computer scanning technology, some of those charred pieces of paper are giving up their secrets at the center, where archivists are hard at work reconstructing the past.

You can also request the records of numerous celebrities, political figures, and other noteworthy names who served in the military, including Jackie Robinson, Jimmy Stewart, or Henry Kissinger. And, yes, there are local favorites as well. Jack Buck and Stan Musial both served in uniform.

The largest individual military record belongs to Gen. Henry Arnold, whose Air Force file clocks in at more than 6,000 pages.

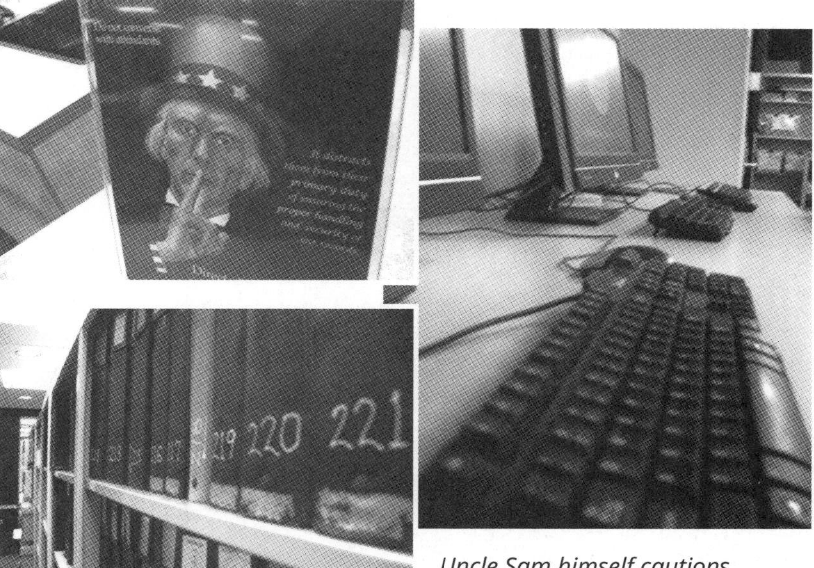

Uncle Sam himself cautions patrons to remain quiet while in the research rooms of the National Personnel Records Center. The facilities are open to the public by appointment and are a favorite with everyone from professional historians to amateur genealogists. Under federal regulations, military records become available to the general public 62 years after an individual's separation from service in uniform.

94 THE NOT-SO-DISMAL SCIENCE

Where can you find a million-dollar money cube in St. Louis?

If you've ever been told that something "looks like a million bucks," there just happens to be a place in town where you can actually put a visual to the time-honored cliché. Welcome to the Inside the Economy Museum at the Federal Reserve Bank of St. Louis.

Economics may be nicknamed "the dismal science," but no one tries to jazz it up quite like the local Fed, which has created something resembling a fiscally oriented version of the Magic House. A trip through this museum will find you awash in multimedia presentations, electronic games, and futuristic graphics that could, at times, rival a laser-light show, all dedicated to explaining currency supply, consumer goods, commodities trading, and every other aspect of the miracle that is capitalism. While topics like "How inflation

INSIDE THE ECONOMY MUSEUM

WHAT A million-dollar museum

WHERE 1 Federal Reserve Bank Plaza

COST Admission is free, which seems odd for an institution dedicated to teaching capitalism

NOTEWORTHY The St. Louis Fed covers all or part of seven states.

The "Money Cube" shows what a million bucks would look like in singles which, on reflection, is almost certainly not the best way to carry it around.

affects you" may seem a bit dry, the sleek, illuminated panels, high-tech interactive displays, and scrolling, market-style readouts make this institution of learning feel as though the *Starship Enterprise* went through a corporate merger with the New York Stock Exchange.

And yes, there really is a giant money cube out front so you can drool over truly Bill Gatesian quantities of dough. You don't get to keep the moolah of course. But they say the pleasure of a great museum is priceless, and you can even pick up a nice little bag of shredded cash as a souvenir on your way out.

One dollar bills with the letter "H" in the seal denote St. Louis as the issuing Federal Reserve Bank.

From the moment you enter its sliding glass doors, the benefits of the free market come alive for guests at the Inside the Economy Museum at the Federal Reserve Bank of St. Louis.

95 A DIFFERENT KIND OF WATER PARK

What is so historic about this water tower?

Viewed at a distance along Interstate 44, the Compton Hill water tower actually looks a bit like a strange brick rocket ship ready to take off and hurtle skyward toward the wild blue yonder.

But the real story is significantly cooler than that. This structure is one of only seven "standpipe"-style water towers in the entire United States. The standpipes were erected as a device to maintain water pressure in old public plumbing systems.

Perhaps more amazing, there are two others right here in town. Those are both in traffic circles on the Northside—a weathered white column on Grand Avenue and a vividly red structure at the intersection of Bissell Street and Blair Avenue.

The 179-foot Compton Hill structure is unique in a number of ways. For starters, it isn't surrounded by a road like its cousins but rather by a park, which also encompasses a massive raised and walled structure. This is a huge reservoir

---

The smaller tower along the side of the main shaft is designed to shunt overflow water out of the standpipe if it were to fill.

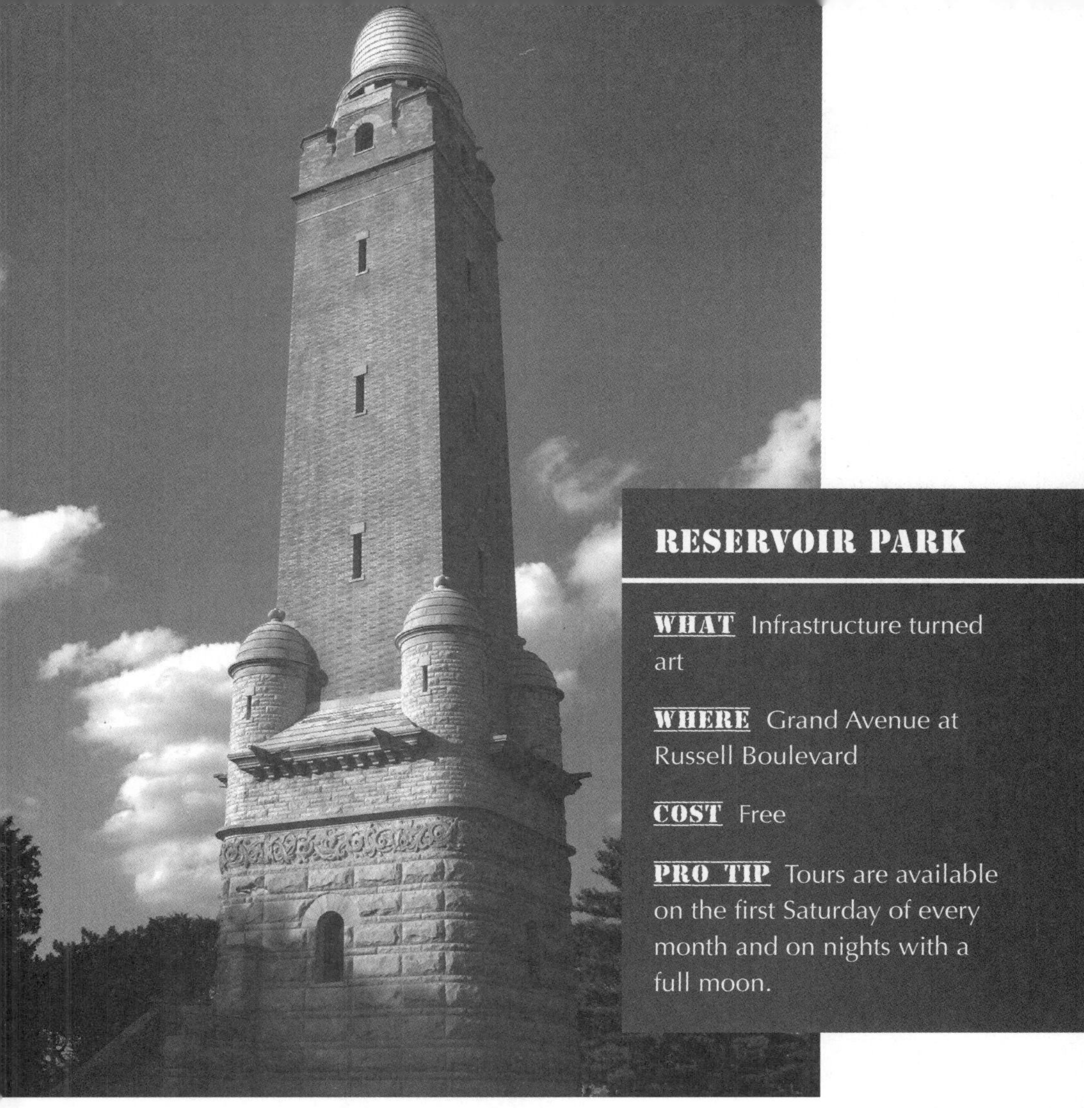

RESERVOIR PARK

WHAT Infrastructure turned art

WHERE Grand Avenue at Russell Boulevard

COST Free

PRO TIP Tours are available on the first Saturday of every month and on nights with a full moon.

This architectural marvel is really just the shell for a large standpipe that once helped to regulate water pressure.

that was built just after the Civil War. The inside contains a tank capable of holding 28 million gallons of water. Its corresponding tower was completed in 1899.

Today, the restored Compton Hill tower still stands as the centerpiece for one of St. Louis's most unique and interesting parks.

96 THE TRUTH HURTS

What was so scandalous about this Southside statue that it nearly resulted in legal action?

Sometimes philanthropy doesn't always turn out the way the donor would like. Adolphus Busch may have paid for most of this statue, but when he requested that she cover up, designer Wilhelm Wandschneider had a simple enough answer for his benefactor.

No.

It is an ethos that seems to sum up *The Naked Truth,* which depicts a topless young woman holding torches aloft. That may seem tame enough today, but in 1914 it was still considered something of a scandal. The controversy was so substantial that Wandschneider had to threaten to sue if he wasn't paid.

The Naked Truth was dedicated in honor of three editors for the German-American St. Louis Westliche Post newspaper.

THE NAKED TRUTH

WHAT Truth, beauty, and the controversy those things often engender

WHERE Grand Avenue at Russell Boulevard

COST None

NOTEWORTHY *The Naked Truth* originally cost $31,000 to create.

Sitting in quiet repose in Reservoir Park, a disrobed Truth is as much a St. Louisan as anyone.

Even the *Post-Dispatch* "Weatherbird" took note of the nude figure's victory over her detractors when the sculpture was narrowly voted in by a panel tasked with deciding the issue.

But winning came at a cost, and there was a catch. The statue's dark appearance is no accident. She was cast in bronze rather than marble in the belief that a bright white figure would do too much to accentuate her attributes.

Ultimately, she may also have been the victim of unfortunate geopolitical timing. She was erected by the German-American Alliance, and the twin torches in her hands represent those two nations. Within three years of the statue's dedication, they would be at war with each other.

97 HARRY'S BIG MOMENT

Where was one of the most iconic political photos of all time taken?

It is probably the most famous still photograph in all of American electoral history. A victorious Harry Truman holds up a copy of the *Chicago Tribune*, grinning broadly as he waved it to throngs of cheering supporters.

The headline says it all. "DEWEY DEFEATS TRUMAN," it blasts in bold black letters across the front page, in one of journalism's most ignominious errors.

But while the paper may have come from Chicago, the photo didn't. It was actually taken right here in St. Louis. Truman, the only Missourian to ever be elected to the highest office in the land, was standing in none other than our very own Union Station. The crowd of thousands joining him in a laugh at the *Tribune's* expense were St. Louisans. Truman had been on his way back east from his home in Independence, and he'd been tossed the paper when his train stopped at Union Station.

UNION STATION

WHAT A newspaper's worst moment and a politician's best

WHERE Union Station

COST The *Chicago Tribune's* self-respect

NOTEWORTHY St. Louis's three newspapers at the time—the *Post-Dispatch*, the *Star-Times*, and the *Globe-Democrat*—all endorsed Dewey.

The fellow who handed the famous paper to Truman was C. Arthur Anderson, a congressman from South County.

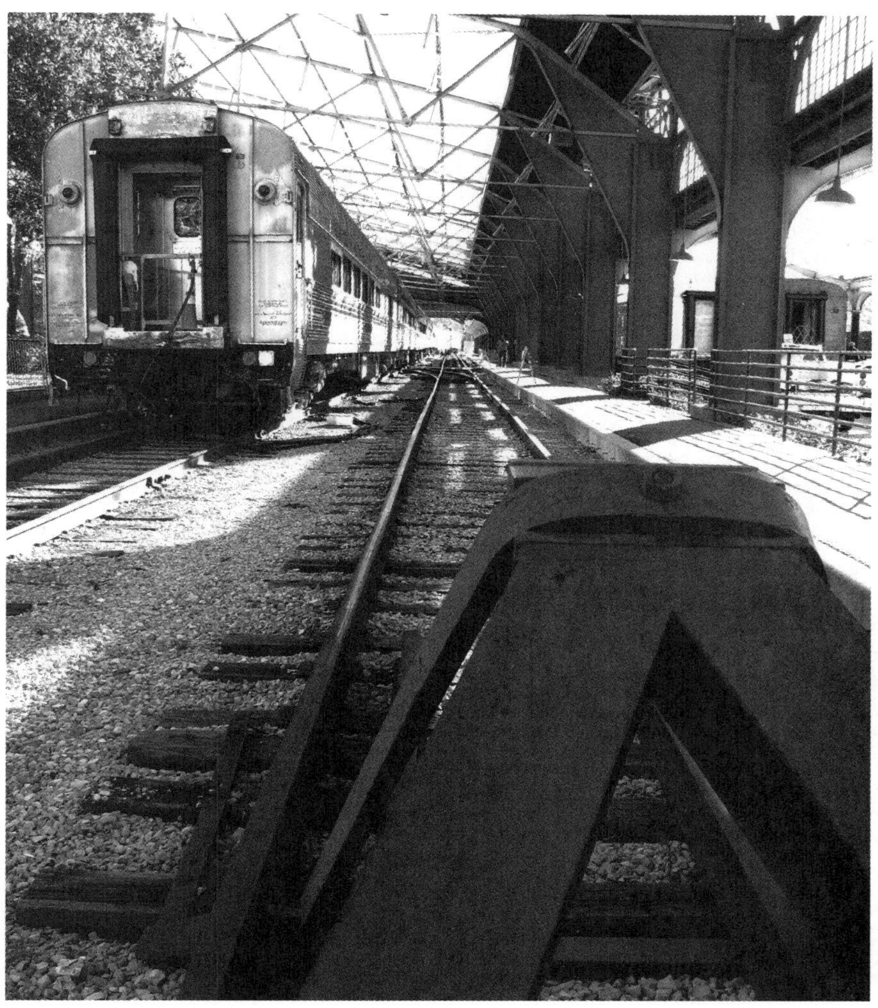

Truman's finest hour happened right here on old Track 32 when political journalism's most embarrassing mistake was immortalized for the ages on film.

Surprisingly, the photo's location doesn't get a lot of fanfare. Union Station is no longer a train depot. Now it is a popular shopping venue. No signs mark the spot where Truman's train stopped and his many supporters cheered but it actually lies along the stretch of track closest to 20th Street on the station's west side.

St. Louis shoppers still pass the area every day on bargain-hunting expeditions—most blissfully unaware of what happened there.

BIBLIOGRAPHY

1. **The Big Cone:** "HOUR STORY: A quest for big things" *Suburban Journals*. July 19, 2012. By Scott Bandle. http://www.stltoday.com/suburban-journals/metro/life/hour-story-a-quest-for-big-things/article_b786a431-6942-5479-b878-8ec23c6dc39a.html
2. **The Phantom Freeway:** "The life and death of the American urban interstate as told by St. Louis' I-755" NextSTL. May 18, 2015. By Brendan Wittstruck. http://nextstl.com/2015/05/the-life-and-death-of-the-american-urban-interstate-as-told-by-st-louis-i-755/; "Missouri highway log and Missouri terminus gallery" KCRoads via Internet Archive Wayback Machine. https://web.archive.org/web/20021224072351/, http://www.kcroads.com/ShowMe/MOTerm/755.html; "St. Louis street index" St. Louis Public Library. http://www.slpl.lib.mo.us/libsrc/c-street.htm
3. **BIGFOOT® Hangs His Hat in Pacific:** "The history of BIGFOOT" Bigfoot 4x4. http://bigfoot4x4.com/blog/?page_id=364
4. **The Bizarre Battle of Hermann:** "Hermann Civil War video: Story of the little cannon" YouTube.com Nov. 17, 2011. Uploaded by Hermann Chamber of Commerce. https://www.youtube.com/watch?v=s3tmRB2bXNc; "'Living history' farm in Hermann opens with commemoration of Civil War skirmish. *St. Louis Post-Dispatch*. Sept. 18, 2011. By Tim O'Neil. http://www.stltoday.com/news/local/metro/living-history-farm-in-hermann-opens-with-commemoration-of-civil/article_3370b14c-cb38-571f-8025-cc1159f96011.html
5. **Drawing Outside the Lines:** Information from site visit.
6. **The Broken Heart of West County:** "Creve Coeur history" City of Creve Coeur. http://www.creve-coeur.org/index.aspx?nid=220 "Creve Coeur Park History" St. Louis County. http://www.stlouisco.com/Portals/8/docs/Document%20Library/parks/PDFs/ParkHistory/CreveCoeurHistory.pdf; "Creve Coeur Lake Memorial Park" St. Louis Audubon Society. http://www.stlouisaudubon.org/conservation/cclmp.php
7. **The Staircase to Nowhere:** "Fort Belle Fontaine" St. Louis County. http://www.stlouisco.com/ParksandRecreation/ParkPages/FortBelleFontaine; "Autumn wanderings, Part 2: Fort Belle Fontaine" *St. Louis Magazine*. Nov. 14, 2012. By Thomas Crone http://www.stlmag.com/news/Autumn-Wanderings-Part-2-Fort-Belle-Fontaine/
8. **American Graffiti:** "State of street art: Vandalism or legit, it's not going away" *Riverfront Times*. Jan. 21, 2009. By Keegan Hamilton. http://www.riverfronttimes.com/stlouis/state-of-street-art-vandalism-or-legit-its-not-going-away/Content?oid=2453330; "Paint Louis 2015" Paint Louis. http://www.stlpaintlouis.com/; "Paint Louis in jeopardy after graffiti artists 'bomb' St. Louis" *Riverfront Times*. Sept. 22, 2015. By Jeremy Essig. http://www.riverfronttimes.com/newsblog/2015/09/22/paint-louis-in-jeopardy-after-graffiti-artists-bomb-st-louis
9. **Escape From Missouri:** "Chain of Rocks Bridge" National Park Service. http://www.nps.gov/nr/travel/route66/chain_of_rocks_bridge_illinois_missouri.html
10. **Picnic at the Toxic Waste Dump:** "Weldon Spring Site Interpretive Center and educational opportunities online tour" Department of Energy, Office of Legacy Management. http://www.lm.doe.gov/Weldon/Interpretive_Center/Online_Tour.pdf " Army Reserve buildings open at old TNT site in Weldon Spring" *St. Louis Post-Dispatch*. Oct. 24, 2014. By Jesse Brogan. http://www.stltoday.com/news/local/govt-and-politics/army-reserve-buildings-open-at-old-tnt-site-in-weldon/article_2f3dcf16-130d-5dae-b631-2c4f9cf855ca.html; "A pile of nuclear waste now a tourist attraction in Weldon Springs, Missouri" Amusing Planet. May 28, 2013. By Kaushik. http://www.amusingplanet.com/2013/05/a-pile-of-nuclear-waste-now-tourist.html; "GWOU administrative record section title: GW-800-801-1.21" Department of Energy. http://www.lm.doe.gov/Weldon/GW-800-801-1_21.pdf Information from site visit.
11. **KSHE's Suburban Roots:** "KSHE station history" St. Louis Media History Foundation. By Frank Absher. http://www.stlmediahistory.com/index.php/Radio/RadioArticles/kshe-station-history; "Ed Ceries" St. Louis Media History Foundation. By Frank Absher. http://www.stlmediahistory.com/index.php/Radio/RadioHOFDetail/ceries; "In Concert: KSHE and 40+ Years of Rock In St. Louis" By John Neiman. Big Jack Publishing. 2009. http://www.stlbook.com/pages/1960s/mike.html
12. **Mound at the Musial:** "Welcome to Mound City" Missouri History Museum Blog. Dec. 12, 2013. By Caoimhe Ni Dhonaill. http://www.historyhappenshere.org/node/7480; "A look back: Big Mound in St. Louis, legacy of a lost culture, leveled in 1869" *St. Louis Post-Dispatch*. Nov. 12, 2013. By Tim O'Neil. http://www.stltoday.com/news/local/metro/look-back/a-look-back-big-mound-in-st-louis-legacy-of/article_3b006339-444d-575f-91c5-8b4f96fa08cd.html; "Metropolitan life on the Mississippi" *Washington Post*. Mar. 12, 1997. By Nathan Seppa. http://www.washingtonpost.com/wp-srv/national/daily/march/12/cahokia.htm
13. **Diamond in the Rough:** "A diamond interchange with a twist" The Official Website of the DDI. http://www.divergingdiamond.com/; "History of Maryland Heights" Maryland Heights Convention and Visitors Bureau. http://www.more2do.org/history/
14. **The Battle of St. Louis:** "The Battle of Fort San Carlos" *Distilled History*. Jun. 5, 2013. By Cameron Collins. http://www.distilledhistory.com/battlefortsancarlos/
15. **Never Again:** "Holocaust Museum looks forward on 20th anniversary" *St. Louis Jewish Light*. Aug. 12, 2015. By David Baugher. http://www.stljewishlight.com/news/local/article_9b2b3b28-410d-11e5-872b-a7bfa017bdee.html; "About HMLC" Holocaust Museum and Learning Center in Memory of Gloria M. Goldstein. http://hmlc.org/
16. **Peace, Love, and . . . Bargains:** "Under the Dove: A Collection of Memories" By Lynne Lang. Imagine That Enterprises L.C., 2002
17. **Half a Highway:** "Environmental impact statement" Southcountyconnector.com. http://www.southcountyconnector.com/about.html; "Interstate 244" Interstate-guide.com. Updated Aug. 20, 2014. http://www.interstate-guide.com/i-244_mo.html
18. **Smallpox Island:** "Smallpox Island" Alton Convention & Visitors Bureau. http://www.visitalton.com/business/detail/332/smallpox-island; "Visitors guide to the Confederate prison site & Confederate memorials" Great River Road. http://www.greatriverroad.com/cities/alton/confederate.htm; "Confederate POW burials on Smallpox Island, West Alton" USGenWeb Archives. http://www.usgwarchives.net/mo/civilwar/smallpox.htm

19. **The Ghosts of Times Beach:** "Around the nation: Times Beach, Mo., votes itself out of existence" *New York Times*. Apr. 3, 1985. http://www.nytimes.com/1985/04/03/us/around-the-nation-times-beach-mo-votes-itself-out-of-existence.html; "In Missouri, a battle over burying a toxic town" *New York Times*. May 30, 1990. By William E. Schmidt. http://www.nytimes.com/1990/05/30/us/in-missouri-a-battle-over-burying-a-toxic-town.html; "Remember Times Beach: The dioxin disaster, 30 years later" *St. Louis Magazine*. Dec. 3, 2012. By William Powell. http://www.stlmag.com/Remember-Times-Beach-The-Dioxin-Disaster-30-Years-Later/
20. **The Ghosts of Times Beach, Part 2:** "Meramec River, U.S. 66 Bridge" National Park Service. http://www.nps.gov/nr/travel/route66/meramec_river_us_bridge_66.html
21. **The National's First No-No:** "July 15, 1876: Wearin' of the 'grin': George Bradley's no-hitter" Society for American Baseball Research By Parker Bena. Originally in "Inventing Baseball: The 100 Greatest Games of the 19th Century" 2013. Edited by Bill Felber. http://sabr.org/gamesproj/game/july-15-1876-wearin-grin-george-bradleys-no-hitter; "Sportsman's Park, Busch Stadium I" Project Ballpark. http://www.projectballpark.org/history/na/busch1.html "Sportsman's Park" Ballparks of Baseball. http://www.ballparksofbaseball.com/past/SportsmansPark.htm; "1876 St. Louis Brown Stockings" Baseball-Reference.com. http://www.baseball-reference.com/teams/STL/1876-schedule-scores.shtml
22. **A River Doesn't Run Through It:** "Early Settlers" City of Des Peres. http://www.desperesmo.org/Index.aspx?NID=183; "Des Peres History" City of Des Peres. http://www.desperesmo.org/Index.aspx?NID=181
23. **Mirrored Maplewood:** "Maplewood public art" City of Maplewood. https://mo-maplewood.civicplus.com/index.aspx?NID=277; "History" City of Maplewood. http://www.cityofmaplewood.com/index.aspx?NID=102
24. **Strollin' Zombie Road:** "Five St. Louis ghost stories that just won't die" *Riverfront Times*. Oct. 25, 2012. By Leah Greenbaum. http://www.riverfronttimes.com/stlouis/five-st-louis-ghost-stories-that-just-wont-die/Content?oid=2501495; "Rock Hollow Trail" TrailLink by Rails-to-Trails Conservancy. http://www.traillink.com/trail/rock-hollow-trail.aspx; "After hours, Zombie Road is haunted by police and trespassers" *St. Louis Post-Dispatch*. Oct. 31, 2011. By Matthew Hathaway. http://www.stltoday.com/news/local/metro/after-hours-zombie-road-is-haunted-by-police-and-trespassers/article_71018496-7ff3-5eaa-8def-7118eab24141.html
25. **Where the Coral Court Lives On:** "Coral Court: The no-tell motel with a touch of class" www.coralcourt.com http://www.coralcourt.com/main.html Information from site visit.
26. **The Invisible Town:** "The Champ" *Riverfront Times*. Feb. 14, 2001. By Laura Higgins. http://www.riverfronttimes.com/stlouis/the-champ/Content?oid=2483294; "Bill Bangert dies, 'world's strongest mayor' created Champ" *St. Louis Post-Dispatch*. July 15, 2011. By Michael D. Sorkin. http://www.stltoday.com/news/local/metro/bill-bangert-dies-world-s-strongest-mayor-created-champ/article_79624cf4-353e-5e5f-b4c9-595fffeee048.html; "Spring Break in Champ, Mo" Better Together. By Joe Wilson. http://www.bettertogetherstl.com/spring-break-in-champ-mo
27. **Birth of a Beverage:** "7Up" www.snopes.com. Updated Apr. 27, 2014. By Barbara Mikkelson. http://www.snopes.com/business/names/7up.asp; "Vess soda bottle" Mound City on the Mississippi. http://stlcin.missouri.org/history/structdetail.cfm?Master_ID=2210; "Best orange soda: Vess Whistle orange" *Riverfront Times*. http://www.riverfronttimes.com/stlouis/best-orange-soda/BestOf?oid=2508409; "Charles Leiper Grigg: Soft drink inventor" Missouri Legends. http://www.missourilegends.com/business-and-technology/charles-leiper-grigg/
28. **For the birds . . . :** "Birding in Riverlands" Audubon Center at Riverlands. http://riverlands.audubon.org/birding-riverlands; "Trails in Riverlands" Audubon Center at Riverlands. http://riverlands.audubon.org/trails-riverlands; "Unique partnership" Audubon Center at Riverlands. http://riverlands.audubon.org/unique-partnership
29. **Circle of the Seasons:** "Woodhenge" Cahokia Mounds State Historic Site. http://cahokiamounds.org/explore/#tab-id-8; "World Heritage List" UNESCO World Heritage Centre. http://whc.unesco.org/en/list/; "Visitors guide to the Woodhenge" Great River Road. http://www.greatriverroad.com/somadco/collins/woodhenge.htm
30. **The Legendary Lion:** "History" Lion's Choice. http://www.lionschoice.com/about-us/history; "FAQ" Lion's Choice. http://www.lionschoice.com/about-us/faq
31. **The Hidden Cemetery:** "History of the shrine" Old St. Ferdinand Shrine. http://www.oldstferdinandshrine.com/shrine-history/ Information from site visit.
32. **The Ultimate Sacrifice:** "The 'lucky' ship in Pearl Harbor" *Washington Post*. Dec. 10, 1981. By Alan M. Schlein. https://www.washingtonpost.com/archive/local/1981/12/10/the-lucky-ship-in-pearl-harbor/fbbb7d0a-a399-4486-8edb-946d08656191/; "Soldiers Memorial" University of Missouri-St. Louis. http://www.umsl.edu/virtualstl/phase2/1930/buildings/soldiers%20memorial.htm; "History of the Soldiers Memorial" City of St. Louis. http://www.stlsoldiersmemorial.org/index.php?option=com_content&view=article&id=54&Itemid=29
33. **The Giant Eyeball:** "Tony Tasset" Laumeier Sculpture Park. http://www.laumeiersculpturepark.org/tony-tasset/; "The odyssey of Chicago's new Eye sculpture" *Chicago Tribune*. July 3, 2010. By Lauren Viera. http://articles.chicagotribune.com/2010-07-03/entertainment/ct-ae-0704-tony-tasset-eye-main-20100702_1_sparta-chicago-loop-alliance-giant-eyeball; "Tony Tasset's three-story eyeball" Interview. Nov. 1, 2013. By Rachel Small. http://www.interviewmagazine.com/art/tony-tasset-dallas-eye/#_
34. **Mary of the Mississippi:** "History of the shrine" Our Lady of the Rivers Shrine. http://ourladyoftheriversshrine.org/
35. **Origins of the Freeway:** "Three states claim first Interstate highway" Public Roads. Summer 1996. By Richard F. Weingroff. https://www.fhwa.dot.gov/publications/publicroads/96summer/p96su18.cfm; "Documentation of the historic Blanchette Bridge over the Missouri River" Missouri Department of Transportation. By Karen L. Daniels. Oct. 2012. http://library.modot.mo.gov/RDT/reports/historicbridges/Blanchette%20Bridge%20L0561%20Documentation.pdf
36. **If the Shoe Fits:** "Brown Shoe to rebrand itself as Caleres" *St. Louis Post-Dispatch*. Apr. 16, 2015. By Lisa Brown. http://www.stltoday.com/business/local/brown-shoe-to-rebrand-itself-as-caleres/article_b02a5fdc-ac37-5343-8570-42fc973b0b4c.html; "Brown Shoe Company" *St. Louis Post-Dispatch*. Apr. 16, 2015. By Karen Elshout. http://www.stltoday.com/brown-shoe-company/image_efc80fae-008a-5232-8869-42ea4bc15dc7.html; "I spy with Rick Graefe" *Suburban Journals*. Oct. 9, 2007. By Rick Graefe. http://www.stltoday.com/suburban-journals/i-spy-with-rick-graefe/article_215f8bbd-e911-5b42-9e7f-5aa47c7cfe9d.html; "Our history" Washington University. http://brownschool.wustl.edu/About/Pages/History.aspx

37. **School's In:** "The history of the Carondelet Historical Society" Carondelet Historical Society. http://www.carondelethistory.org/about-us.html; "A preservation plan for St. Louis Part I: Historic contexts" City of St. Louis. Sept. 1995. By Jeffrey E. Smith. https://www.stlouis-mo.gov/government/departments/planning/cultural-resources/preservation-plan/Part-I-Education.cfm; "America's first kindergarten" Watertown Historical Society. http://www.watertownhistory.org/articles/kindergardenfirst.htm; "Susan Elizabeth Blow" University of Missouri. By Carlynn Trout, Valerie Kemp and Jillian Hartke. http://shs.umsystem.edu/historicmissourians/name/b/blow/ Information from site visit.

38. **The Great Bird of Alton:** "The Legend of the Piasa Bird" Ghost Stories from Haunted Alton. By Troy Taylor. http://www.altonhauntings.com/piasa.html; "Piasa legend is pure fiction!" Jon's Southern Illinois History Page. By John J. Dunphy. http://www.illinoishistory.com/piasabird.html; "Piasa bird" Atlas Obscura. By MattB. http://www.atlasobscura.com/places/piasa-bird; "The Piasa: Monstrous mascot" *Roadside America*. http://www.roadsideamerica.com/story/37106; "The Piasa Bird" *Roadside America*. http://www.roadsideamerica.com/story/12165

39. **Making Tracks on Hodiamont:** "A look back: Hodiamont Line streetcar closed out 107 years of service" *St. Louis Post-Dispatch*. May 23, 2010. By Tim O'Neil. http://www.stltoday.com/news/local/metro/a-look-back-hodiamont-line-streetcar-closed-out-years-of/article_3656e70d-0610-5592-90bc-7deebd14331f.html; "The end of the Hodiamont streetcar right-of-way" UrbanReview Saint Louis. May 21, 2012. By Steve Patterson. http://www.urbanreviewstl.com/2012/05/the-end-of-the-hodiamont-streetcar-right-of-way/

40. **Daniel Boone Slept Here:** "History of Ritenour" Ritenour School District. http://www.ritenour.k12.mo.us/pages/Ritenour_School_District/Alumni/History_of_Ritenour Information from site visit.

41. **Fame in 64 Squares:** "WCHOF History" World Chess Hall of Fame. http://www.worldchesshof.org/about/about-the-hall-of-fame/wchof-history/ Information from site visit.

42. **The World Comes to St. Louis:** "Our accomplishments" Chess Club and Scholastic Center of St. Louis. http://saintlouischessclub.org/about-us/our-accomplishments Information from site visit.

43. **Sherman's Pride:** "Air National Guard planes moving from Lambert to Whiteman AFB" *St. Louis Post-Dispatch*. Mar. 31, 2015. By J.B. Forbes. http://www.stltoday.com/gallery/news/air-national-guard-planes-moving-from-lambert-to-whiteman-afb/collection_00a36141-22ae-531c-9b51-ab780fdeccab.html#0; "Bangert Park" City of Florissant. http://www.florissantmo.com/egov/apps/locations/facilities.egov?view=detail&id=11; "The M-4 Sherman Tank was hell on wheels – and a death trap" Real Clear Defense. Oct. 26, 2014. By Paul Huard. http://www.realcleardefense.com/articles/2014/10/26/the_m-4_sherman_tank_was_hell_on_wheels_-_and_a_death_trap.html Information from site visit.

44. **This Old Church:** "Holy Family Catholic Church" Holy Family Catholic Church. http://www.holyfamily1699.org/

45. **Eliza Hoole is Not Buried Here:** "Tombstones for Trees" The American Mercury. Mar. 1959. By Ruth Louise Johnson. http://www.unz.org/Pub/AmMercury-1959mar-00013; "Historical overview" TowerGrovePark.org Revised Mar. 2002. http://www.towergrovepark.org/index.php/history/historical-overview.html

46. **The Ruins of St. Louis:** "Henry Shaw" TowerGrovePark.org. http://www.towergrovepark.org/index.php/history/henry-shaw.html; "Entrances" TowerGrovePark.org. http://www.towergrovepark.org/index.php/history/entrances.html; "Landscape" TowerGrovePark.org. http://www.towergrovepark.org/index.php/history/landscape.html; "March 30" Joe Sonderman's YesterdaySTL . . . By Joe Sonderman via STLMedia.net. ©Joe Sonderman http://www.stlmedia.net/sonderman/march/03-30hist.pdf

47. **Birth of the Billiken:** "What is a Billiken? Unmasking SLU's cool and unusual mascot" St. Louis University. Aug. 9, 2011. http://www.slu.edu/evgrn-what-is-a-billiken?DB_OEM_ID=27200; "Billiken history" Church of Good Luck. http://www.churchofgoodluck.com/Billiken_History.html; "Billikens used to hit the gridiron" The University News. Oct. 30, 2008. By Jonathan Ernst. http://www.unewsonline.com/2008/10/30/billikensusedtohitthegridiron/; "Bud Billiken" www.budbillikenparade.org. http://www.budbillikenparade.org/; "What is a Billiken?" St. Louis University. Nov. 12, 2015. http://www.slu.edu/what-is-a-billiken

48. **The Big Apple:** "A little history about the Blue Owl!" The Blue Owl Restaurant and Bakery. By Mary Hostetter. http://theblueowl.com/index.php/our-story; "The history of Kimmswick" www.visitkimmswick.com. http://visitkimmswick.com/history Information from site visit.

49. **Kimmswick's Bed of Bones:** "The Kimmswick Bone Bed" Missouri Department of Natural Resources. https://mostateparks.com/page/54983/general-information; "What's the difference between a mammoth and a mastodon?" Mental Floss. Dec. 19, 2013. By Mark Mancini. http://mentalfloss.com/article/54120/whats-difference-between-mammoth-and-mastodon

50. **St. Louis County's First Road:** "Riverwoods Park and Trail" City of Bridgeton. Updated Oct. 3, 2015. http://www.bridgetonmo.com/departments/parks-and-recreation/parks/riverwoods-park-trail; "History of the City of St. John" City of St. John. http://www.cityofstjohn.org/index.php/history-of-st-john.html; "Early beginnings: The St. Charles Road & the gateway to the Santa Fe Trail" The Wellston Loop. http://www.thewellstonloop.com/early-beginnings-the-st-charles-road-the-gateway-to-the-santa-fe-trail

51. **Liberty Throughout the Land:** "Jewish Tercentenary Monument" Forestparkstatues.org. http://www.forestparkstatues.org/jewish-tercentenary-monument/

52. **Tortoise Time:** "Turtle playground" Forestparkstatues.org. http://www.forestparkstatues.org/turtle-playground/; "'Sunny' Glassberg dies; philanthropist who donated Turtle Park" *St. Louis Post-Dispatch*. May 20, 2013. By Michael D. Sorkin. http://www.stltoday.com/news/local/obituaries/sunny-glassberg-dies-philanthropist-who-donated-turtle-park/article_4ca2eb2b-852e-5171-910e-03949009c1bf.html; "Turtle Monument" Forestparkstatues.org. http://www.forestparkstatues.org/turtle-monument

53. **Just Barge Right In:** "Lock tours" Meeting of the Rivers Foundation. http://www.meetingoftherivers.org/html/lock_tours.html; "Melvin Price Locks & Dam" U.S. Army Corps of Engineers. http://www.mvs.usace.army.mil/Missions/Navigation/LocksandDams/MelvinPrice.aspx; "Representative Melvin Price, 83, is dead of cancer after 22 terms" *New York Times*. Apr. 23, 1988. By Jesus Rangel. http://www.nytimes.com/1988/04/23/obituaries/representative-melvin-price-83-is-dead-of-cancer-after-22-terms.html; "Visitors guide to the Melvin Price Locks & Dam" *Roadside America*. http://www.greatriverroad.com/cities/ealton/melvinprice.htm

54. **Five Borders in 45 Seconds:** "St. Louis County Municipal League" St. Louis County Municipal League. http://www.stlmuni.org/

55. **Abe Lincoln's Swordfight:** "Smallpox Island" Alton Convention and Visitors Bureau. http://www.visitalton.com/business/detail/332/smallpox-island; "The time Abraham Lincoln and a political rival almost dueled on an island" Mental Floss. Sept. 18, 2014. By Julia Davis. http://mentalfloss.com/article/12382/time-abraham-lincoln-and-political-rival-almost-dueled-island

56. **Erudition Along the Back Nine:** "University officials claim Bugg Lake unofficial" The Current. Nov. 9, 1989. By Thomas Kovach. http://www.umsl.edu/~libweb/university-archives/Student%20Newspaper/Current,%201987-1989/1989/November%209,%201989.pdf; "From golf balls to hallowed halls" University of Missouri-St. Louis archives. http://www.umsl.edu/library/archives/Exhibits/From%20Golf%20Balls%20to%20Hallowed%20Halls/buildings%20and%20grounds.html

57. **Think Locally, Label Globally:** "FAQ" Earth City Levee District.http://earthcityld.com/faq.aspx Interview with Sam Basilico of Earth City Business Park.

58. **Lord of the Rivers: The Two Towers:** "Hey Heidi: What are those Miss. River castles?" KSDK-TV. Sept. 25, 2014. By Heidi Glaus. http://www.ksdk.com/story/news/local/hey-heidi/2014/09/25/mississippi-river-castles-chain-of-rocks/16194179/; "Rare glimpse inside Mississippi River water intake towers" Fox2News. Feb. 13, 2015. By Patrick Clark. http://fox2now.com/2015/02/13/rare-glimpse-inside-mississippi-river-water-intake-towers/; "Our aging water infrastructure" Metro Water Infrastructure Partnership via the City of Kirkwood website. Aug. 2014. By primary author Nicole A. Young. http://www.kirkwoodmo.org/mm/files/Water/2015/MWIP%20Report%20on%20Aging%20Infrastructure%20August%202014.pdf

59. **The Gentle Giant:** "Robert Pershing Wadlow" www.altonweb.com. Updated Oct. 1998. http://www.altonweb.com/history/wadlow/

60. **Taking Flight:** "Boeing and McDonnell Douglas tie $48 billion knot" *Christian Science Monitor*. Dec. 16, 1996. http://www.csmonitor.com/1996/1216/121696.us.us.1.html; "James S. McDonnell Prologue Room in St. Louis" Boeing. http://www.boeing.com/company/tours/prologue-room.page

61. **Confluence–East:** "About" Lewis & Clark Confluence Tower. http://www.confluencetower.com/about

62. **Confluence–West:** "Columbia Bottom Conservation Area" Missouri Department of Conservation. http://mdc.mo.gov/regions/st-louis/columbia-bottom-conservation-area

63. **The Boots of O'Fallon, MO:** "Veterans Memorial Walk" City of O'Fallon. http://www.ofallon.mo.us/veterans-memorial-walk; "Military Times lists O'Fallon, Missouri, as a great place for veterans to live" City of O'Fallon. Jul. 6, 2015. By Peggy Whetzel. https://www.ofallon.mo.us/News/military-times-lists-o-fallon-missouri-as-a-great-place-for-veterans-to-live

64. **The Star of O'Fallon, IL.:** "O'Fallon Veterans' Monument, O'Fallon, Ill" www.ofallonveteransmonument.org. http://www.ofallonveteransmonument.org/

65. **The Great Debate:** "Looking for debate zingers? It started with Lincoln and Douglas" National Constitution Center. Aug. 4, 2015. http://blog.constitutioncenter.org/2015/08/looking-for-debate-zingers-it-started-with-lincoln-and-douglas/

66. **Collinsville's Colossal Condiment:** "The world's largest catsup bottle" The World's Largest Catsup Bottle Official Web Site and Fan Club. http://www.catsupbottle.com/

67. **Respect for Rover:** "About us" The American Kennel Club Museum of the Dog. http://www.museumofthedog.org/about_us.html

68. **The Other St. Louis Arch:** "About" St. Louis Union Station. http://www.stlouisunionstation.com/about/ Information from site visit.

69. **The Universe in a Few Easy Steps:** "Delmar Loop Planet Walk" Loopplanetwalk.com. http://loopplanetwalk.com/

70. **A True Breadwinner:** "Panera's Rosenthal cashes in" *St. Louis Business Journal*. Jan. 5, 2010. By Christopher Tritto. http://www.bizjournals.com/stlouis/stories/2010/01/04/story2.html; "Panera's CEO Ron Schich recalls spinoff of bread company" *St. Louis Business Journal*. Jan. 14, 2013. By E.B. Solomont. http://www.bizjournals.com/stlouis/blog/2013/01/paneras-ceo-ron-shaich-recalls.html; "Our history" Panera Bread. https://www.panerabread.com/en-us/company/about-panera/our-history.html; "Winfield's Gathering Place" Winfield's Gathering Place. http://winfields.net/

71. **Multiple McKinleys:** "KETC/Living St. Louis/McKinley Bridge" YouTube.com. Jan. 14, 2008. Uploaded by Nine Network. https://www.youtube.com/watch?v=D-5uxXZazzQ&feature=channel&hl=en&gl=IL; "McKinley Bridge" www.johnweeks.com. By John A. Weeks, III. http://www.johnweeks.com/river_mississippi/pagesC/umissC03.html; "McKinley Bridge" Built St. Louis. http://www.builtstlouis.net/industrial/mckinley-bridge.html

72. **St. Charles County's Piece of 9/11:** "9-11 memorial: A tribute to first responders" City of O'Fallon.http://www.ofallon.mo.us/9-11-memorial

73. **Where a King Spoke:** "Rabbi Jerome W. Grollman dedicated 60-year career to beliefs, principles" United Hebrew Congregation Bulletin. Oct. 2008. http://www.unitedhebrew.org/Libraries/PDF_s/Grollman_Bulletin_-_Final_Layout.sflb.ashx; "Finding Dr. Martin Luther King, Jr. in St. Louis" Preservation Research Office. Jan. 21, 2013. By Michael R. Allen. http://preservationresearch.com/2013/01/finding-dr-martin-luther-king-in-st-louis/; "Library" Missouri History Museum. http://mohistory.org/lrc/collections/library; "Objects" Missouri History Museum. http://mohistory.org/lrc/collections/objects; "Our building" Missouri History Museum. http://mohistory.org/lrc/your-visit/faqs/our-building

74. **Supreme Injustice:** "Dred Scott case: The Supreme Court decision" PBS: Africans in America. http://www.pbs.org/wgbh/aia/part4/4h2933.html; "Dred Scott" The State Historical Society of Missouri: Historic Missourians. http://shs.umsystem.edu/historicmissourians/name/s/scottd/

75. **The Man Who Made Georgia Howl:** "Telegram of William T. Sherman to Ulysses S. Grant, October 9, 1864" North Carolina State University. http://cwnc.omeka.chass.ncsu.edu/items/show/143; "Insiders' Guide: Civil War Sites in the South" Fourth Edition. Revised and updated by Shannon Hurst Lane. P. 139. Morris Book Publishing. 2010; "Columbia mileposts–Aug. 11, 1880: Even if 'war is hell' Sherman didn't say exactly that in his famous speech" *Columbus Dispatch*. Aug. 11, 2012. By Gerald Tebben. http://www.dispatch.com/content/stories/local/2012/08/11/even-if-war-is-hell-sherman-didnt-say-exactly-that-in-his-famous-speech.html
76. **Brews and Bibles:** "History" Humphrey's Restaurant & Tavern. http://www.humphreysstl.com/history/; "Who we are" The Gathering. http://www.gatheringnow.org/who-we-are/
77. **The Designs of Youth:** "Hoosiers & Scrubby Dutch: St. Louis's South Side. Second Edition." By Jim Merkel. Reedy Press. 2014. https://books.google.com/books?id=M7pGCgAAQBAJ&pg=PT45&lpg=PT45&dq=william+ittner+merkel&source=bl&ots=RvZh6TtDUE&sig=WYuJCdxBw47otDirc_phknQKs_c&hl=en&sa=X&ved=0ahUKEwi_zMy8zM7JAhXITSYKHVKECL8Q6AEIHDAA#v=onepage&q=william%20ittner%20merkel&f=false; "The St. Louis schools of William B. Ittner" Distilled History. Aug. 30, 2012. By Cameron Collins. http://www.distilledhistory.com/ittnerschools/
78. **Keys to the City:** "Honey, Where's My Metro Pass? art installed at St. Charles Rock Road MetroLink station" NextStop – The Official Blog of Metro Transit – St. Louis. Jul. 13, 2010. By Courtney. http://www.nextstopstl.org/2541/honey-wheres-my-metro-pass-art-installed-at-st-charles-rock-road-metrolink-station/; "MetroLink celebrates 20 years of light-rail service" *St. Louis Post-Dispatch*. Jul. 26, 2013. By Ken Leiser. http://www.stltoday.com/news/traffic/along-for-the-ride/metrolink-celebrates-years-of-light-rail-service/article_9fa1d2d2-22fa-5dfb-96e0-8982d9d7c520.html
79. **In the Buff . . . :** "Forty Acre Club: America's Gateway Family Nudist Resort" Forty Acre Club. http://www.fortyacreclub.com/ Information by interview.
80. **The Roots of Government:** "Thomas Hart Benton" Architect of the Capitol. http://www.aoc.gov/capitol-hill/national-statuary-hall-collection/thomas-hart-benton
81. **Career Liftoff:** "Obama calls LaunchCode of St. Louis a national model" *St. Louis Post-Dispatch*. Mar. 10, 2015. By Lisa Brown. http://www.stltoday.com/business/local/obama-calls-launchcode-of-st-louis-a-national-model/article_550685f8-ca36-51c4-814d-17b93ee80a29.html; "LaunchCode" LaunchCode. https://www.launchcode.org/
82. **The Indian of Cherokee Avenue:** "Cherokee sculptor is his own worst critic" *Suburban Journals* Jun. 1, 2007. By Jim Merkel. http://www.stltoday.com/suburban-journals/cherokee-street-sculptor-is-his-own-worst-critic/article_c1a4b734-e38e-506b-a85e-5e2bede43963.html
83. **Chain Reaction:** "Arch Reactor" Arch Reactor. https://archreactor.org/
84. **Rome of the West:** "Visitors Guide: Cathedral Basilica of Saint Louis" Cathedral Basilica of Saint Louis. http://cathedralstl.org/wp-content/uploads/Cathedral-Basilica-Stl-Brochure-English.pdf
85. **A Rail Worker's Delight:** "City history" City of Eureka, http://www.eureka.mo.us/government/city-history/
86. **Metallic Mystery:** "Re-envisioning Richard Serra's 'Twain.'" Sculpture City. Mar. 24, 2014. By Meridith Mckinley. http://sculpturecitystl.com/journal/re-envisioning-richard-serras-twain/; "Serra Sculpture Park amenities" City of St. Louis. https://www.stlouis-mo.gov/government/departments/parks/parks/browse-parks/view-park.cfm?parkID=111&parkName=Serra%20Sculpture%20Park&amenitySubTypeID=27#amenity480; "Portrait/homage/embodiment" Pulitzer Foundation for the Arts. http://portrait.pulitzerarts.org/courtyard/joe/
87. **The Still Life:** "Laclede's Landing Wax Museum" Laclede's Landing Wax Museum. http://stlwaxmuseum.com/
88. **An Unpleasant Awakening:** "The Awakening" Regional Arts Commission. http://racstl.org/public-art/the-awakening/; "Chesterfield: Sculptures throughout city grab viewers' attention" *Suburban Journals*. Aug. 25, 2009. By Mary Shapiro. http://www.stltoday.com/suburban-journals/metro/news/chesterfield-sculptures-throughout-city-grab-viewers-attention/article_d146feca-01c3-5dea-917c-d8b7c1f426b4.html; "Art at National Harbor" National Harbor. http://www.nationalharbor.com/art-at-national-harbor/
89. **Miracle on 11th Street:** "Miracle of St. Peter Claver" Shrine of St. Joseph. http://www.shrineofstjoseph.org/miracle.html
90. **Queen of the Drive-In:** "Missouri drive-ins" Roadside Architecture. http://www.roadarch.com/driveins/mo.html; "Skyview Drive-In" Skyview Drive-In. http://www.skyview-drive-in.com/
91. **Being a Bit Velodramatic:** "Penrose Park Velodrome – St. Louis" Penrose Park Velodrome. http://penroseparkvelo.com/
92. **Hazelwood to the High Court:** "Facts and case summary – Hazelwood v. Kuhlmeier" United States Courts. http://www.uscourts.gov/educational-resources/educational-activities/facts-and-case-summary-hazelwood-v-kuhlmeier; "About Hazelwood East High" Hazelwood School District. http://www.hazelwoodschools.org/SchoolsAndPrograms/High%20Schools/HazelwoodEastHighSchool/Pages/HazelwoodEastHighHistory.aspx
93. **Recording Heroism:** "The National Personnel Records Center (NPRC)" National Archives. https://www.archives.gov/st-louis/; "The National Archives at St. Louis" Commemorative issue from *St. Louis Post-Dispatch* advertising. Oct. 2011.
94. **The Not-So-Dismal Science:** Information from site visit.
95. **A Different Kind of Water Park:** "The water towers of St. Louis" Distilled History. May 7, 2012. By Cameron Collins. http://www.distilledhistory.com/watertowers/; "Compton Hill Reservoir Park: A little-known St. Louis landmark" Examiner. Jun. 23, 2011. By Edward Farrell. http://www.examiner.com/article/compton-hill-reservoir-park-a-little-known-st-louis-landmark
96. **The Naked Truth:** "Naked Truth shines brightly again in Reservoir Park" Examiner. May 20, 2014. By Amy Borrelli. http://www.examiner.com/article/naked-truth-shines-brightly-again-reservoir-park; "Naked Truth statue" The Water Tower & Park Preservation Society. http://www.watertowerfoundation.org/naked_truth_history.asp
97. **Harry's Big Moment:** "A look back: Truman called memorable photo 'one for the book'" *St. Louis Post-Dispatch*. Nov. 1, 2009. By Tim O'Neil. http://www.stltoday.com/news/local/govt-and-politics/a-look-back-truman-called-memorable-photo-one-for-the/article_bb74ebfa-1828-53dd-b7a6-8bf1eac3ea95.html

All internet sources accessed as of Dec. 16, 2015.

INDEX